THE HOUSE OF THE LORD

*God's Plan to
Liberate Your City
From Darkness*

FRANCIS FRANGIPANE

Creation House
Lake Mary, Florida

THE HOUSE OF THE LORD by Francis Frangipane
Published by Creation House
Strang Communications Company
600 Rinehart Road
Lake Mary, FL 32746
Web site: http://www.creationhouse.com

Unless otherwise noted, Scripture quotations are from the
New American Standard Bible. Copyright © 1960, 1962, 1963,
1968, 1971, 1972, 1973, 1974, 1977 by the Lockman
Foundation. Used by permission.

Scripture quotations marked AMPLIFIED are from the Amplified
Bible. Old Testament Copyright © 1965, 1987 by the
Zondervan Corporation. The Amplified New Testament
Copyright © 1954, 1958, 1987 by the Lockman Foundation.
Used by permission.

Scripture quotations marked KJV are from the King James
Version of the Bible.

Scripture quotations marked LB are from The Living Bible.
Copyright © 1971. Used by permission of Tyndale House
Publishers, Inc., Wheaton, IL 60189. All rights reserved.

Library of Congress Catalog Card Number: 91-70020
International Standard Book Number: 0-88419-284-9

8 9 0 1 2 3 4 5 BBG 13 12 11 10 9 8
Printed in the United States of America

"How awesome is this place!
This is none other than the house of God,
and this is the gate of heaven."
Genesis 28:17

ACKNOWLEDGMENTS

Special thanks to Marilyn Bryant and Kevin Dwyer, without whose help the completion of this manuscript would have been improbable. Also, I want to thank our friends at Creation House for their patience and flexibility with us. My deepest appreciation to my wife and children whose willing sacrifice and support gave me the liberty to devote myself to this project.

CONTENTS

PART FOUR—Our Strategy: Obedience to Christ

FOREWORD

*E*verywhere I go I hear of the contribution of Francis Frangipane. In the past few months, pastors and other spiritual
leaders have gathered in prayer in historically large numbers. Most
of these gatherings are citywide and encompass the whole spectrum
of Christian movements and ministries.

Our concern is to bring revival and healing to our cities. There have
to be answers. Most of our churches are not growing. There is only
a small harvest among youth, and our children continue to be raised
in an atmosphere of spiritual oppression.

The answers cannot simply be new innovations. We are turning to
the bedrock of God's Word with a hunger to rediscover the ageless
principles whereby a land is healed.

This book is a timely and valuable contribution that has caused me to think deeply on God's character and ways. But more than that it is a wonderfully encouraging word of wisdom for the church of the nineties.

My spirit resonated in agreement as I turned these pages. I recommend this work as a needed companion to the book *Taking Our Cities for God*. Today's spiritual leaders must receive these insights. Here are the answers we have cried out for, clearly stated and biblically based. This excellent book will stand the test of time.

John Dawson
Los Angeles, California
January 1991

PREFACE

It will take a citywide church to win the citywide war. Our separate, isolated efforts will not stop the flood of increasing evil in our cities if we, as Christ's church, remain isolated from each other. You may challenge that thought, but it was none other than Jesus Himself who said, "Any city or house divided against itself shall not stand" (Matt. 12:25).

In a universal and true sense, every Christian is part of the Lord's eternal house. Practically speaking, however, the house of the Lord is only functional as we are "built together," where the church becomes "a dwelling of God in the Spirit" (Eph. 2:19-22). Therefore we have taken the liberty in this book to define the house of the Lord as that living, united, praying church in the city. The Lord's house will consist of evangelicals and Pentecostals, traditional churches and charismatics; it will be free of racial and class prejudices. They will simply be Christians in the city who know Jesus as Lord, believe the truth of the Scriptures and are committed to one another as brethren. Although they will continue to maintain their national affiliations and identities, they will be uniquely anointed to bring healing to their communities.

Yes, revival is coming. But we should be forewarned: this moving of God will not impact every city. Areas where the church is yet divided will be bypassed; darkness will continue to increase in such areas. Indeed, in most cases the obstacle hindering revival will not only be the devil; it will be the stronghold of religious pride and self-contentment in the church. Let us remember with sobriety the warning of John the Baptist: "Every mountain and hill shall be brought low" (Luke 3:5).

Like all rivers, the eternal river of life *avoids* mountains. Yet it flows naturally into valleys and plains. Before we will ever be truly prepared for the Lord Jesus, the mountain of our pride must come down. It is a fact worth noting that, in preparation for Christ, God placed John the Baptist in the Jordan Valley. This valley is actually the lowest place in the world. The Lord began His greatest work in the lowest place on earth. Indeed, all those whom the Lord will empower will pass through a valley of lowliness.

At the same time, if it seems as though God has been ignoring your church or that you are too lowly to be used, remember that John's message also encouraged: "Let every valley and ravine be filled and lifted up" (Is. 40:4; Luke 3:5). If you have felt like a valley amidst the apparent mountains of God, know that as you are connected with the other churches in the city for prayer, the ultimate intention of the Lord is that you be filled and lifted up before His return.

God will give grace to the humble, and together they will bring a new purity to Christianity. They will speak with lasting credibility of Christ's forgiveness; they will be examples of His love toward one another.

Yes, we are greatly encouraged. For we are seeing a tremendous moving of the Spirit of God as He prepares His church for the coming harvest. In hundreds of cities the Lord has raised up thousands of pastors; these leaders are meeting together regularly in prayer for each other and their cities. This work is God's, and He Himself is the source of our great hope. The very fact that this book is in your hands and that you desire to see the church in your city become the house of the Lord is an indication of the grace of God.

Indeed, prior to Jesus' coming *for* His church it is our vision that He will be revealed *in* His church. To His glory this book is committed and dedicated.

Francis Frangipane
December 1990

PART ONE

Cleansing
the Lord's House

How little we understand of the One who has
granted us the unfathomable riches of His presence!
We are called to be His house, His place of rest.
Yet not until we are cleansed of sin
will His purposes for us become clear;
not until we are pure will we see God.

"And they assembled their brothers, consecrated themselves,
and went in to cleanse the house of the Lord,
according to the commandment of the king
by the words of the Lord."
2 Chronicles 29:15

ONE

Cleansing the Holy Place

*W*ithin *every Christian there is a secret place, a sanctuary we must prepare for the Lord. This holy place is not unlike the holy of holies in the Jewish temple. Not until this place is cleansed will the Lord dwell within us in the fullness of His Spirit; not until this room is pure will we truly become a house for the Lord.*

Bring Out the Unclean Thing

"And it was for this He called you through our gospel, that you may gain the glory of our Lord Jesus Christ" (2 Thess. 2:14). The Lord is cleansing us for the distinct purpose of bringing His people into His glory. Out of His desire to present a pure bride to His Son, the Father is purging the church of its sin. He is refusing to allow

17

our interchurch relationships to continue without love. According to the Scriptures, before Jesus returns the body of Christ will be holy and blameless (see Eph. 5:27; Titus 2:14; 1 Thess. 5:23; Col. 1:22; Phil. 2:15; and others). Through new and successive levels of purity, the house of the Lord will again see and reflect the glory of God.

To facilitate this process of cleansing, by way of example, we will study one of the greatest periods of restoration and renewal in the Bible: the rule of King Hezekiah. Prior to Hezekiah's reign, his father, King Ahaz, brought the very worst forms of idolatry into Israel. Ahaz shut the temple doors and persecuted the priests. Those whom he did not kill he corrupted. Without the influence of a godly priesthood Israel soon followed Ahaz into idolatry and unrestrained sin.

Although Hezekiah was a relatively young man when he succeeded Ahaz as king, he was God's anointed man to bring revival and healing to the nation. In the very first month of his reign he "opened the doors of the house of the Lord and repaired them" (2 Chron. 29:3). He then consecrated the priesthood and began to restore the temple. Hezekiah's first priority was for true worship to be established. We read, "And he brought in the priests and the Levites, and gathered them into the square on the east. Then he said to them, 'Listen to me, O Levites. Consecrate yourselves now, and consecrate the house of the Lord' " (2 Chron. 29:4-5).

God initiated His plan to redeem the nation by consecrating the priests and cleansing the house of the Lord. For this task Hezekiah had been prepared. As a young man he watched Israel's "fathers...fallen by the sword." The men who were not slain on the battlefield could be heard weeping in the grainfields: "our sons and our daughters and our wives are in captivity" (2 Chron. 29:9). Hezekiah knew only one option, one plan, was offered to Israel: return to God. In obedience, he began his reign by consecrating the house of the Lord.

Hezekiah next ordered the priests to "carry the uncleanness out from the holy place." Before the eternal One moves visibly in power, He moves invisibly in holiness. He cleanses His house. Then the outward signs of restoration and revival, the miracles and true conversions, can come forth. If God will touch our cities with His fire, He must put that fire within us. Everything the Almighty does for us as individuals will in time bless His church and work to fulfill His eternal purpose in our nation. He will deliver those who are not innocent, and they will be delivered through the cleanness of our hands (Job 22:30).

Hezekiah reopened and cleansed the temple. He never stopped thinking of Israel but knew he must begin with a consecrated priesthood. It is significant that he made no appeal or effort to win the nation itself; he had no program of reform other than reinstituting true worship. The king's focus was not on turning the heart of the people but drawing the heart of God. If the Lord is lifted up, He will of His own will and power draw all men unto Himself.

Even as Hezekiah reopened the temple doors, so also in us there is a door which we must open daily to the Lord. David wrote, " 'I was always beholding the Lord in my presence' " (Acts 2:25). Right there within the psalmist's heart was a dwelling place for the Lord; David was always beholding the Lord. Similarly, there is something in our presence, in our spirits, which can be opened or closed to God. We must not assume that because we are Christians this gate toward God is automatically opened. Jesus stood "at the door" of the church in Laodicea and knocked, desiring to enter their lives. We must choose to unlock this door and swing it wide toward Christ.

Yet opening this chamber of our hearts can indeed be a frightening thing. For it requires that we be open to talk to God and to hear from Him as well. It is one thing for us to speak honestly with the Lord; it is quite another when He speaks without restraint to us. Therefore, the most essential commodity for stimulating revival is a tender, open heart before God.

Is the door of your heart opened toward God? Can the Spirit of Jesus Christ come in and speak with you? Are you defenseless to His voice? Can you sense both His pleasure and His displeasure? For us to become sensitive to divine realities we must live with the door of our hearts open. It is impossible to do the will of God otherwise.

King Hezekiah commanded the priests to carry the uncleanness out from the holy place. The call to clean the holy place was not an option; it was a command. "So the priests went in to the inner part of the house of the Lord to cleanse it, and every unclean thing which they found in the temple of the Lord they brought out to the court of the house of the Lord" (2 Chron. 29:16).

When the priests entered the holy place, they entered alone; the rest of Israel was in the outer court and beyond. Here, privately before God, they were to remove those things which were defiling this sacred place. No one else had seen these desecrations. They could have remained in secret, and none except the priests would have known; but they did not. They brought out the unclean things. What was unholy was exposed publicly and removed.

From where did these abominations arise? Predominantly they were the sins of their forefathers—the traditions and offenses handed down to them from the wicked generation which preceded them. The careless approach to holiness, the unbelief toward the promises of God, the idolatry and worship of man-made things were the products of a generation turned from God. They gave to their children, as a legacy, a society oppressed by sin and the devil.

In the new-covenant temple, the church, it is our private, inner life which needs this deep cleansing. We have inherited traditions which justify and reinforce darkness of soul within us. Most Christians have little hope that purity of heart is even attainable. The revival which will turn a nation begins in the trembling unveiling of our hearts, in the removal of what is defiled and hidden within us.

I will tell you a mystery. It is in this very place, this chamber of our deepest secrets, that the door to eternity is found. For if the Father is near enough to "see in secret," He is close enough to be seen in secret as well. If He has entered us, we can, in truth, enter Him. The key to entering the presence of God is intimacy, and intimacy is secrets shared. To ascend the hill of the Lord, to stand in the holy place, we must have clean hands and a pure heart; we cannot lift up our souls toward falsehood (see Ps. 24:3-4). At this door of eternity we must renounce those things hidden because of shame and, in humility of soul, receive Christ's cleansing word.

The Pure in Heart See God

Our goal is not merely to be "good" but to see God and, in seeing Him, to do what He does. However, John tells us that he who seeks to "see Him just as He is...purifies himself, just as He is pure" (1 John 3:2-3). We can be assured that each step deeper into the Lord's presence will reveal areas in our hearts which need to be cleansed. Do not be afraid. When the Spirit shows you areas of sin, it is not to condemn you but to cleanse you.

Let me give you an example: My wife set herself apart to seek the Lord. Her cry during this time was, "Lord, I want to see You." As she sought the Lord, however, He began to show her certain areas of her heart where she had fallen short. She prayed, "Lord, this is not what I asked for; I asked to see You, not me." Then the Holy Spirit comforted her, saying, "Only the pure in heart can see God."

In the same way the Lord desires His church to see Him as well. Thus, He is exposing the areas in us which are unclean. If we will walk as Jesus walked, we must remember that Christ did only the things He saw the Father do (John 5:19). Out of the purity of His heart He beheld God and then revealed His glory.

The purpose of consecrating the priesthood and cleansing the house of the Lord is that we might sincerely be prepared for more of Christ. This cleansing must become a way of life, but it does not have to take a lifetime. For Hezekiah and the people with him, it occurred in a matter of eight days.

"Thus the service of the house of the Lord was established again. Then Hezekiah and all the people rejoiced over what God had prepared for the people, because the thing came about suddenly" (2 Chron. 29:35-36). The key here is this: The cleansing of the temple was the highest priority of the king's life. When we set our hearts toward true holiness, we too will "rejoice over what God [has] prepared."

There is yet one more thought, a postscript to this message. The prophet Malachi also tells us that the Lord "whom you seek, will suddenly come to His temple" (Mal. 3:1). As we restore the house of the Lord to purity and cleanse the holy place of our hearts for

21

Christ, He will indeed come "suddenly" into our midst. After the Lord in His fullness returns to His house, He promises, "Then I will draw near to you for judgment; and I will be a swift witness against the sorcerers and against the adulterers and against those who swear falsely, and against those who oppress the wage earner in his wages, the widow and the orphan, and those who turn aside the alien, and do not fear Me" (Mal. 3:5).

When the Lord is in His house, He will release judgment upon our cities. Wickedness will be cut off, and our cities will be healed in His presence.

Blessed Lord, I desire deeply for You to dwell in me. I yearn to be Your holy dwelling place. I ask that the sanctuary of my heart be purged of every defilement of flesh and spirit (2 Cor. 7:1). Here they are, Lord Jesus, my hidden sins. I bring them out of the secret chamber of my heart. (Audibly identify your sins by name.) I take them out of the darkness and expose them to Your light. You have promised You will execute Your word upon the earth, thoroughly and quickly. O God, thoroughly cleanse my heart; purify me quickly! In Jesus' name, amen.

TWO

The Building
Site of the
Temple

T *he building of the house of the Lord involves more than finding help in our time of need. There are costs to attaining God's best. If we want to have His greatest provisions, we must yield to Him our greatest loves.*

Our Greatest Loves

The Scriptures refer to two types of temples: one made of stone, which was built in Israel, and the other made of flesh, which is the church. The first temple, Solomon's, was built at a predetermined site which God selected. Even as the Lord carefully chose the building site for the temple of stone, so He is looking at the landscape of our hearts, seeking to make us His temple of flesh. Two important events were instrumental in designating the temple site. These events developed over many years but were nevertheless a composite of what we ourselves must become. The first is found in the life of Abraham.

The Lord brought Abraham to a place of spiritual fulfillment in his son, Isaac. But a time came when it was required of Abraham to choose between his love for God and his love for what God had given him. The Lord commanded Abraham to take his son to the land of Moriah. There Abraham was told to offer Isaac on the mountain of God's choosing.

"On the third day Abraham raised his eyes and saw the place from a distance. And Abraham said to his young men, 'Stay here with the donkey, and I and the lad will go yonder; and we will worship and return to you' " (Gen. 22:4-5). Notice Abraham's last statement, "we will worship and return." We see here the perfection of faith in the atmosphere of worship. Abraham's faith told him they would both return, but it was his attitude of worship which enabled him to go up. The story is well-known. The angel of the Lord stopped Abraham, knife in hand, from taking Isaac's life. Yet it was within the plan and purpose of God to require obedience of His servant. Abraham's love for God was tested and proven true.

Likewise, to qualify for the house of the Lord, the first attitude we must possess is a worshipping heart; we must be willing to give to God what we love the most. For pastors it may be surrendering personal dreams concerning their ministry or their churches. For intercessors it may be giving up their role of leadership in a local prayer group in order that those praying might be integrated into a larger corporate body.

In death every man ultimately surrenders all he owns to God. Those who are called to build Christ's house do so by surrendering their highest loves and their very desire of fulfillment to the Almighty. It is a death not unlike the death of the flesh. Hope of human recovery is abandoned; the sense of trust abides alone in God. Abraham offered to God his greatest love, Isaac, who was the embodiment of his spiritual fulfillment. He laid all his dreams upon an altar he built with his own hands.

Abraham was willing to trust God to fulfill His promises, knowing that death is no barrier to the Almighty. So also those whom God chooses as the building site of His house will give to God what they have loved the most. Within their yielding, worshipping hearts, He will build His house.

The Full Price

In the next scene we find David. He is standing upon a mountain-top overlooking Jerusalem; his sin has brought the Lord's displeasure upon the nation. In response to his repentance David is told to build an altar to the Lord on Ornan's threshing floor. The mountain upon which David is standing is Mt. Moriah, the same place where, six centuries earlier, Abraham offered Isaac to God.

Although Ornan freely volunteered his oxen for the sacrifice and his ox yoke for the fire, David refused. He said, "For the full price you shall give it to me, that the plague may be restrained from the people...I will surely buy it for the full price; for I will not take what is yours for the Lord, or offer a burnt offering which costs me nothing" (1 Chron. 21:22-24).

In contrast to what has been typical of our American approach to God's call, here again we behold the nature of those in whom the house of the Lord is built. They are not looking for shortcuts in their service to God; they refuse to give that which is another's. Rather these yielded souls pay the full price, refusing to offer the Lord that which costs them nothing.

Let me add this: On Mt. Moriah Abraham had a revelation of the nature of God. He called this place, which would ultimately become the site of Solomon's temple, "Jehovah-Jirah": The Lord will provide. From that time it was said, "In the mount of the Lord it will be provided" (Gen. 22:14).

Many Christians wonder why, if "provider" is the nature of God, they receive so little response from Him. The answer is partly because the provisions of God are not given randomly or to support our selfish inclinations. Rather, *"in the mount of the Lord it will be provided."* In truth, the provisions of God are without limit to those

25

who give their all to Him. For on the building site of the temple, where His house is built, there will be an abundance.

Dear Lord, I desire to be given fully to You. Forgive me for offering costless sacrifices and borrowed gifts. Jesus, I want to pay the full price. I know the issue is not what I can do for You, but what You can make of me. I surrender my all to You. May the quality of my life be suitable for Your house. And grant me a heart of faith and worship to bring my Isaac to the altar. In Jesus' name, amen.

THREE

Obtaining the Endorsement of God

*I**f we will gain God's greatest blessings, we must embrace His highest purpose.*

The Workmanship of God: Christlikeness

The theme of this book is building the house of the Lord. Our sincere conviction is that if this dwelling place of God emerges in our cities it will transform entire regions, and great revival will break out. However, if our goal is anything other than becoming a home for Jesus, this truth will become another "wind of doctrine"; we will be blown off course again. Without the abiding fullness of Christ in the church we will have no more impact in the world than a political party, whose strength rests in numbers and not in God.

Consequently, every serious Christian must recognize two priorities. We need to return to the simplicity and purity of devotion to Christ; and we desperately need divine intervention, or our nation will perish.

In Psalm 90 Moses utters a prayer that everyone who has had enough of his own feeble efforts should pray. In somber and earnest supplication he implores, "Let Thy work appear to Thy servants, and Thy majesty to their children. And let the favor of the Lord our God be upon us; and do confirm for us the work of our hands; yes, confirm the work of our hands" (Ps. 90:16,17).

This is a heartfelt prayer, one that is full of deep thought and candid reflection. Moses was not willing to "try something" and ask the Lord to bless it. He prayed, "Let *Thy* work appear." He appealed to God to confirm the works of his hands. What is divine confirmation? It is when the Lord works with you and upholds your words with His power (Mark 16:20; Heb. 2:4). God identifies Himself so fully with what you are doing that He backs you up with power. It is the endorsement of the Almighty upon an individual's life.

I want to underscore that we have peace with God through Christ's sacrifice. We are not looking for divine acceptance but divine endorsement. The question is not one of salvation but of power in this life to change our world. How then can we truly know that we have found God's highest purposes for us? How can we, like Moses, obtain the endorsement of almighty God?

If we want our works to have permanence, then they must be the eternal works of God and not more of man's ideas. Jesus said, "For the works which the Father has given Me to accomplish, the very works that I do, bear witness of Me, that the Father has sent Me" (John 5:36). Ultimately we only glorify God when we, like Jesus, accomplish the work which He has given us to do (John 17:4).

You may ask, Does God have eternal, enduring assignments *for me?* Yes, but the first "work of God" that is accomplished in us is not our work but His, that we "believe in Him whom He has sent" (John 6:29). We must abandon all hope of finding true spiritual success apart from dependent, steadfast faith in the Person and power of Christ.

This forsaking of our ideas to embrace simple obedience to Christ is the "work of God." We must see that we cannot attain to the works of God unless we first become the workmanship of God. "For we are His workmanship, created in Christ Jesus for good works, which God prepared beforehand, that we should walk in them" (Eph. 2:10). At this very moment there are eternal, powerful works prepared for each of us. Yet, until we see that the Father's highest purpose is to reveal in us the *nature* of Christ, we will not qualify for the *power* of Christ, which is God's full endorsement upon our lives.

The Mystery of God's Will

If we will find the eternal works of God, we must know His eternal plan. The ultimate plan of God is stated clearly in the Scriptures. Paul wrote, "He made known to us the mystery of His will...with a view to an administration suitable to the fullness of the times, that is, the summing up of all things in Christ, things in the heavens and things upon the earth" (Eph. 1:9-10).

The eternal purpose of God is to sum up all things in Christ, things in the heavens and things upon the earth. He desires to bring the living Christ into each of us as individuals; then, as Christ-filled individuals, we can transform the church. Finally, from the launching pad of a Christ-filled church, we will see "things in the heavens" impacted and cleansed with the Spirit of His Son.

In this unfolding of the Father's plan it is important to note that the expanse of Christ must be accomplished in sequence. That is, we cannot see Christ corporately manifested in the church until we, as individuals, embrace true Christlikeness; nor can we plunder the heavenly places until we unite with other congregations as Christ's church.

God's will is that the church should not be divided but united as a glorious temple, a living house for His Son. God has blessed the church with "every spiritual blessing in the heavenly places" (Eph. 1:3). This realm does not belong to Satan but is part of our inheritance in Christ. It is the eternal wisdom and purpose of God to reveal Christ "through the church"—not only to the world but to

29

the "rulers and the authorities [principalities and powers] in the heavenly places" (Eph. 3:10).

Satan has sought continually to hinder and delay this "summing up of all things in Christ." Yet such is our mission and, in knowing the plan of God, such is our victory. Therefore, in battling for the soul of our cities and our nation, our victory is not in knowing how to command demons, but in knowing the commander Himself. We triumph in being rightly aligned with the supreme plan of God, which is to fill all things with Christ.

Therefore, if we want to obtain the endorsement of God upon our lives, Jesus must become as real to us as the world was when we were sinners. He must become our mind, and we His obedient body. Throughout this book we will continue to establish this vision, which is the Father's singular goal in creation. Our prayer is that by the final chapters you will be incorporated into the purpose of God. As such your life will demonstrate the prepared, eternal works of God; you will attain the quality of life which God Himself can back with power.

Dear Lord, we recognize our desperate and total need of You. How we cry for the restoration of Your fullness to the church! Forgive us for trusting in our programs and ideas; especially pardon us for avoiding You. O God, let Your works appear to Your servants, and Your majesty to our children. Confirm for us the work of our hands; yes, confirm the work of our hands. In Jesus' name, amen.

FOUR

The Credibility Factor

*J*esus *was manifested to destroy the works of the devil. How do we destroy the works of the devil? We must manifest Jesus! The basis of our credibility is Christ revealed in and through us!*

—Reuven Doron

"Are You Not Fleshly?"

Contemporary Christianity looks upon the church in Corinth with unjustifiable smugness. We criticize their carnality, yet can you imagine what Paul would have to say to the church today? He would be outraged by our divisions!

Listen to what Paul wrote to the Corinthians, who were only divided *four* ways! "Now I exhort you, brethren, by the name of our

31

Lord Jesus Christ, that you all agree, and there be no divisions among you, but you be made complete in the same mind and in the same judgment. For I have been informed concerning you...that each one of you is saying, 'I am of Paul,' and 'I of Apollos,' and 'I of Cephas,' and 'I of Christ.' Has Christ been divided?'' (1 Cor. 1:10-13a). The apostle later continued, "For since there is jealousy and strife among you, are you not fleshly, and are you not walking like mere men?'' (1 Cor. 3:3).

Paul then challenged the church, "Do you not know that you are a temple of God, and that the Spirit of God dwells in you?'' (1 Cor. 3:16). We are the temple of God. Our churches, like the stones of the temple, are to be laid side-by-side, building us together "into a dwelling of God in the Spirit'' (Eph. 2:22).

Paul went on to issue a warning to the Corinthians which every Christian should heed. He said, "If any man destroys the temple of God, God will destroy him, for the temple of God is holy'' (1 Cor. 3:17). We have attempted to use this verse to condemn such things as cigarette smoking and sexual vices, and on an individual basis there *are* consequences to these sins. However, Paul is speaking here of more than the sins of excess and pleasure; he is speaking of destroying the *unity* of the temple of God! The apostle warned that if any man destroys the temple through jealousy or sectarianism God will destroy him. The context is speaking plainly in regard to divisions in the church. Paul summarizes his thought by stating, "So then let no one boast in men'' (1 Cor. 3:21).

When pure Christianity degenerates into divided camps of ambitious people, it literally destroys the harmony, power and blessing of the "temple of God.'' The individual who brings or supports such carnal divisions in the church has positioned himself to be judged by God. The temple of God is holy. Our unity together is holy. Our love for one another is holy, for the Father Himself dwells in the resting place of caring attitudes and loving relationships. The warning is severe: "If any man destroys the temple of God, God will destroy him.''

The living God is a God of order; He will not dwell in ruins! Because He is a God of love, He will work with us to rebuild, but

He *will not* sanction our fallen condition with power. He will not lend credibility to our disorder.

When Nehemiah, who was living among the Jewish exiles, heard of the condition of Jerusalem and its temple, he "sat down and wept and mourned for days; and...was fasting and praying before the God of heaven" (Neh. 1:4). The modern Jews also weep as they face the Western Wall, lamenting over the ruins of their temple. Paul mourned when he saw the ruined condition of the Corinthian church. He said, "For I am afraid...that perhaps there may be strife, jealousy, angry tempers, disputes, slanders, gossip, arrogance, disturbances; I am afraid that when I come again my God may humiliate me before you, and I may mourn over many of those who have sinned" (2 Cor. 12:20-21).

This mourning concerning the condition of the Father's house must be in our hearts as well. For we as Christ's church are also in ruins. Yet not only have we failed to mourn our situation, we have not even grasped that we are in ruins! We have "church," but we obviously do not have the living God abiding in power in His temple. How far we have fallen, and how little we know it!

While the redemption of man was always motivating Jesus, His most ardent desire was His zeal for His Father's house; He was "consumed" with it (John 2:17). Building the house of God, the born-again, praying, loving, citywide church, is still Christ's highest priority. The world is His harvest, the church is His bride. His love for the church was the basis of His last recorded prayer: that we would be one. It is still His highest passion today. For until we are united in Him, the world will not believe that God has sent Him (John 17:20-23).

Privileged to Become Christlike

Jerusalem fell to Babylon during Jeremiah's day for many reasons, but underlying them all was the spiritual apostasy of the religious leaders. "The adversary and the enemy could enter the gates of Jerusalem" because of "the sins of her prophets and the iniquities of her priests" (Lam. 4:12-13a). Yes, the city was destroyed by its enemies because the religious leadership failed to bring the people to repentance. They lost the protection of God.

Likewise, sin in Christian leadership today has caused the spiritual death of many around the world. However, before we point the finger, let us examine our own hearts. With greater authority come *less* liberty and privilege. This is a principle we cannot ignore. The path narrows for leadership until our only privilege is to become Christlike in everything.

You see, our cities are in disorder because the church is in disorder. James tells us that where there is jealousy and strife "there is disorder and every evil thing" (James 3:16). Our ambitions have taken our eyes off the will and purposes of God for our cities. We have become jealous of one another. Consequently the disorder, lawlessness and "every evil thing" we see in our society are, at least in part, rooted in the soil of a misdirected and distracted church community.

Because of this the church has lost a measure of its credibility. How can we expect the world to hear our message of love when we, as Christ's body, fail to love each other? We have no right to condemn the world for its pride and arrogance when we, the body of Christ, still refuse to humble ourselves and work with the other churches in our neighborhoods.

Over the years the world has seen many incredible ministries. However, the time of the incredible has passed; the hour for the credible is being established.

Dear Lord, forgive me for thinking I can somehow fake my walk with You, and that You would bless and protect my falsehood. Lord Jesus, I want to be real! I want my relationship with You to be substantial! I pray for the baptism of fire to burn away the scaffolding of empty religious ritual and activity. Let Your power and Your love be the credibility of my life, my home and my church. In Jesus' name, amen.

FIVE

One Purpose: Reveal the Fullness of Christ

*T*he virtue of any institution is not so much in its doctrines or organization; rather its virtue resides in the quality of person it produces.

A New and Fresh Anointing

Some of you have been struggling, not knowing what God has for you. You have been through a season in which the Lord has revealed your need of Him in very dramatic ways. Jesus Himself has been near to you; however, His closeness was not merely in the way of external blessings, but in the way of His cross. Yet you have delighted in this, for the way of the cross has increasingly become the way of your life.

At the same time many of your ideas and programs which once were anointed now seem weak and ineffectual. Even some of your favorite Christian themes, as well as church government in general, have been reduced to a simpler, purer definition of Christianity. You just want to know Jesus. Because this has been God working in you, you are uplifted.

In the midst of the changes you have been through, conviction has grown ever brighter: Your goal is to see the character of Jesus Christ, His meekness, authority and love manifested in your life. You have discovered that any other program or church activity which does not reveal Jesus is a "dead work"; although well-intentioned, these dead works are powerless to transform the people.

The truth is the Holy Spirit is preparing you for a new and fresh anointing from the Lord. Ultimately God will use you to inspire holiness in the church and to shatter the demonic strongholds corrupting your city.

Christlikeness or Christianity?

We have instructed the church in nearly everything but becoming disciples of Jesus Christ. We have filled the people with doctrines instead of Deity; we have given them manuals instead of Emmanuel. It is not difficult to recognize someone from Pentecostal, Baptist or other traditional church backgrounds. Nearly every church seems to develop a particular slant or system of traditions, some of which ultimately obscure the simplicity and purity of devotion to Christ. Submit yourself to their way of thinking and soon you will become like them. Is that wrong? Not necessarily, but for us it will never be enough. We are seeking to be like Jesus, not men; we want the kingdom of God, not typical American Christianity.

Thus, we must be vigilant to submit ourselves passionately and solely to the Spirit and words of the Lord Jesus, incessantly reaching for the holy standards of the kingdom of God. Any focus or goal other than Christ Himself *in fullness* will become a source of deception in the days ahead.

Look at what Jesus did with common men. In just three and a half years average men and women were transformed into fearless disciples, literally filled with the Spirit of God. They did not wince at suffering; they did not withdraw from sacrifice. These ordinary people were equipped with spiritual authority over demons and exercised power over illnesses. They were the living proof that Christ transforms people. Three and a half years of undiluted Jesus will produce in us what it did in them: the kingdom of God! Those men were as average and human as we are. The difference between us and them is Jesus. He is the only difference.

One may argue that this occurred two thousand years ago. True, but "Jesus Christ is the same yesterday and today, yes and forever" (Heb. 13:8). You may say, But they actually heard Jesus speak; they saw His miracles! The same Spirit that worked through Jesus then is poured out upon us today. The Holy Spirit has not grown old and feeble; He has not become apostate. The Spirit is still poured out today. Indeed, the same words Jesus uttered in the first century are still "living and active" in the hearts of men today (Heb. 4:12). Has He not promised to be with us "always, even to the end of the age" (Matt. 28:20)? Jesus is the same; the Holy Spirit is being poured out; and the words of Christ still apply. We have no excuses.

The eternal One who established His kingdom in men two millennia ago is fully capable of producing it in us today. All we need is undiluted, uninhibited Jesus. All we need are hearts that will not be satisfied with something or someone less than Him.

If we argue church government and peripheral doctrines, we will miss completely the true purpose of the church, which is to make disciples of Jesus. Some of you want a pastor; others want elders. Still others will not budge without a deacon's board. A few of you will be unsatisfied until apostles and prophets function interdependently. Let me make it plain: God is not raising up "ministries"; He is raising up bondslaves. After we recognize that the goal is not ministry but slavery, we will begin to see the power of Christ restored to the church.

The pattern for leadership in the years ahead is simple: Leaders must be individuals whose burning passion is conformity to Jesus Christ. Is this not becoming the very passion of your heart, to possess the likeness of Christ? The issue with our churches is not merely one procedure over another; the issue is, will we become people who are seeking hard after Christ?

God can use practically any church structure if the people in that congregation are genuinely seeking Him. On the day before Pentecost He had but a small church of 120 people in an upper room, but they were earnestly seeking God. In Antioch there were prophets and teachers who were together in one heart seeking God (Acts 13:1). When Martin Luther was alive, all the Lord had was a dissatisfied monk, but he was seeking God. The Lord used common men and women in every revival, but first they were seeking God individually.

The outward form is not the issue with the Almighty; the true issue is the posture of the human heart before Him.

Objective Desperation

We may argue church government and procedures, but the truth is that a move of God starts more "formless and void" than structured and well-organized. The desperate, anointed, God-seeking individuals meeting in a basement or an upper room are the ones whom God uses. The Spirit graces them with emptiness, and He pours into their hearts objective desperation. Relentlessly and purposefully they come before God, laying aside their attainments and skills. As Christ emptied Himself, so also they lay aside privileges and comforts and take His form: "the form of a bondservant" (Phil. 2:7).

They then bring their great barrenness to Him, knowing that true fullness is always preceded by true emptiness. They view the knowledge of their spiritual poverty as a gift from God, a preparation for His kingdom (see Matt. 5:3; Rev. 3:17). Is it not true that the greater the sense of emptiness within us, the stronger is our hunger for God?

Those whom God chooses are "new wineskins," cleansed, emptied and capable of expanding with the new wine. Their hearts are containers into which the Spirit of God is poured; they swell with Christ's inner fullness. The purpose of their lives is to contain the fruit and power of the Holy Spirit.

Our approach to God should not be rigidly structured and inflexible but formless and soft. We need to become a people whose heart's passion is to seek God until Christ Himself is actually formed within us (see Gal. 4:19). Therefore, let us not make form or government an issue. The priority is this: Will we lay aside our ideas, return to the Gospels and obey what Jesus commands? Will we become objectively desperate in our search and hunger for God?

Find Jesus, Not Just a Religion

In this new stirring of God, our goal as church leaders and intercessors is to abide in Jesus, not to elevate one denomination above another. John taught, "The one who says he abides in Him ought himself to walk in the same manner as He walked" (1 John 2:6). If we truly abide in Him, we will "walk even as He walked." Are there not a number of areas within each of us where Jesus has become more of a religion than a Person?

The first-century saints had the words of Jesus and they had the Spirit of Jesus. In that simplicity the church enjoyed unsurpassed greatness and power. We also are returning to being His disciples, seeking to walk even as Jesus walked. This is the singular requirement in building the house of the Lord: We must want Christ's image alone established in our hearts.

Is this possible? Are we being reasonable? Listen to what Jesus taught. He said, "He who believes in Me, the works that I do shall he do also; and greater works than these shall he do; because I go to the Father" (John 14:12). He taught, "If you abide in Me, and My words abide in you, ask whatever you wish, and it shall be done for you" (John 15:7). When we are aligned correctly to God's will, we will indeed have the Father's endorsement and the Son's authority.

Therefore, the Father's goal, which must become our goal, is nothing less than Christlikeness, where we become fully trained in the knowledge of the ways of God. The Lord calls us to pay the same price, do the same works and possess the exact same benefits from prayer that Jesus did. We cannot afford to compromise what God has promised, nor disobey what He requires. These verses confirm that when the words of Jesus are taught, and where the Spirit of Jesus has liberty, the life of Jesus is manifested. Let this become both our immediate and our long-term goal: to see Jesus Christ revealed in His fullness in the church.

Dear Lord, forgive us for putting doctrines about church government and administration ahead of our love for You. Cleanse us, Master, of the effects of false religious traditions. Even at this moment grant us unrestrained passion for You and You alone! For Your glory we live and pray. In Jesus' name, amen.

SIX

Unrelenting Love

*T*he Bible describes our relationship with Christ in strong, symbolic pictures of oneness: He is head of a body, husband of a wife, God in His temple. In spite of these powerful metaphors, a sense of distance remains between the presence of the Lord and us. This distance is a test. Our call is to possess that love of God which reaches into eternity and brings the glory and Person of Christ into His earthly house.

Those Who Seek After God

"God has looked down from heaven upon the sons of men, to see if there is anyone who understands, who seeks after God" (Ps. 53:2). We simply must have more of Jesus. In the face of increasing wickedness in the world, our programs and ideas have failed. We need God. Those who understand the hour we face are seeking Him. The wise know that Christ Himself is our only strategy and hope.

You may ask, How does this message fit in the context of building the Lord's house? If just one soul in a city truly attains the hope of this chapter, that individual will change his or her world.

This message is about seeking the Lord. Our text will be from the Song of Solomon 3:1-4, for here we find a bride and bridegroom who both are intolerant of the distance between them. The bride in the passage symbolizes the church in her deepest longings for Jesus; the bridegroom symbolizes Christ. We will start with verse 1; the bride is speaking.

"On my bed night after night I sought him whom my soul loves." True seeking of God is born out of love. Our quest for God is not a matter of discipline but of desire. It is not a question of sacrifice but of undistracted love. Your sleep is gone because your beloved is gone. You must seek Him, for such is the nature of love.

Some will say, "But I already know the Lord. I have found Him." In truth it was He who found us. Our salvation rests securely upon this fact. But while many are resting upon Christ's finding us, His bride arises now to find Him. In the very love which He inspired, she pursues her beloved.

We must see that there is still much more to learn and discover about our Lord. At the end of Moses' life, after being used by God to confront and defeat the gods of Egypt, after dwelling in the Lord's glory for forty years, he prays, "Thou hast begun to show Thy servant Thy greatness and Thy strong hand" (Deut. 3:24). For all we think we know, we have seen but a glimpse of His glory. The apostle Paul wrote, "As many as are perfect, have this attitude" (Phil. 3:15). To seek and know Christ is the attitude of the mature; it is the singular obsession of Christ's bride.

In this maturation process there will come a point when within your heart love for God will take ascendancy over mere intellectual or doctrinal understanding. The bride of Christ cannot contain her longing or patronize her aching heart by saying, "I will feel better in the morning." There is simply no reconciling the passion of her soul with the absence of her beloved.

Note also there is an unfolding dimension to seeking the Lord which we must embrace. Genuine love for God is an unrelenting hunger. As you would die without food, so you feel you will die without Him. She says, "Night after night I sought him." The knowledge of what her beloved has done in the past, a "religion" about Him, will provide little solace for the bride. She wants Him!

Overcoming Resistance

There are many obstacles which hinder us from truly finding the Lord. The bride mourns, "I sought him whom my soul loves. I sought him but did not find him." Her first attempts at seeking her beloved prove fruitless, yet, unlike most of us, she does not terminate her quest. Augustine said it well: "God is not on the surface." There is indeed a "secret place of the Most High." Although hidden, it is accessible.

One common deterrent is the effects of drawing near to the Lord: the blessings of encouragement or a new understanding of Scripture. We must guard against these signposts becoming our final destination. We must not be deterred by goose bumps or tears, edification or comfort. We are searching for Jesus Himself.

Let us also understand we will not find His fullness by seeking Him merely in convenient times and comfortable places. Rather our quest is a determined, continual pilgrimage which will not end until He is disclosed to us (see Phil. 3:12). We are confident, though, for He has promised that, in the day we seek Him with our whole hearts, we shall find Him (see Jer. 29:13).

Christ Our Life

For many, Christianity is simply the religion into which they were born. For others, although Jesus is truly their Savior, their relationship with Him is hardly more than a history lesson, a study of what He did in the past. For those who attain His presence, however, Christ is Savior and more: He is their very life (see Col. 3:4). When

Jesus is your life, you cannot go on without Him.

There is a story of a man in search of God who came to study at the feet of an old teacher. The sage brought this young man to a lake and led him out into shoulder-deep water. Putting his hands upon his pupil's head, he promptly pushed him under the water and held him there until the disciple, feeling he would surely drown, frantically repelled the old man's resistance. In shock and confusion the young man resurfaced. "What is the meaning of this?" he demanded. His teacher looked him in the eyes and said, "When you desire God as you desired air, you shall find Him."

This was the attitude of the psalmist when he wrote, "As the deer pants for the water brooks, so my soul pants for Thee, O God" (Ps. 42:1). The question here is not only of desire but of survival. I need Him as a drowning man needs air and as a parched deer needs water. How can I exist without abiding in the living Christ?

The bride continues, "I must arise now and go about the city; in the streets and in the squares I must seek him whom my soul loves." This inexorable woman has risen from the security of her own bed. She has left the comfort of her warm house and now is seeking her beloved in the streets and in the squares. Pastors, be aware: Not all who wander from church to church are uncommitted or superficial Christians. A significant number are honestly searching for Christ. They are asking, "Have you seen Him?"

Not only is the bride in the streets and squares of Christianity; she is facing the force and the power of darkness as well. Yet nothing stops her—not her own need of sleep nor her fear of the night. The love of Christ compels her.

However, again she is disappointed. "I sought him but did not find him." We might think that after so great an effort—and in the face of the seeming reluctance of heaven to answer her cry—she would feel justified to return home. But she does not. We too must guard against becoming satisfied with our opinion of ourselves: "We prayed; we waited; we searched for God. We did more than other men." This false reward fills the soul with self-exaltation. If we truly want to find Him, we must stay empty and hungry for God alone.

"The watchmen who make the rounds in the city found me, and

I said, 'Have you seen him whom my soul loves?' " From her bed, to the streets and now to the watchmen, the bride is seeking her lover. Notice that the watchmen found her. The watchmen are the modern-day prophetic ministries. Their highest calling is to find the searching bride and direct her to Jesus. While many may come to the seers for a word of encouragement or revelation, the bride is looking for Jesus. Her singleness of purpose is undistracted. She asks the watchmen, "Have you seen Him?"

"Scarcely had I left them when I found him whom my soul loves." This is the greatest motivation for seeking the Lord: The time will come when you find Him! You will pass your tests and overcome the obstacles; you will be secure in the embrace of Christ.

She says, "I held on to him and would not let him go." I am reminded of Mary at the empty tomb of Christ. The apostles came, looked in the cave and went away astounded. But Mary came to the tomb and lingered, weeping. The death of Christ was horrible, but the empty tomb was unbearable. She had to find Him whom her soul loved!

The Scripture says that Jesus Himself came to her, but in her sorrow she did not recognize Him. He said, "Woman, why are you weeping? Whom are you seeking?" Can we see the connection here between Mary's weeping and her seeking Christ? Blinded by her tears, she supposes He is the gardener: " 'Sir, if you have carried Him away, tell me where you have laid Him, and I will take Him away.'

"Jesus said to her, 'Mary!' She turned and said to Him in Hebrew, 'Rabboni!' (which means, Teacher). Jesus said to her, 'Stop clinging to Me, for I have not yet ascended to the Father' " (John 20:15-17).

The instant Mary sees the Lord she clings to Him. Love is the highest, most powerful law of God's kingdom. When you expend your energies, your nights, your heart; when you overcome your fears out of love for Jesus, you will find Him and "never let him go." Mary found Him whom her soul loved. She continued in her pursuit, remaining in sorrow until she found Him. The apostles had gone home. To whom did Jesus appear first? He came to the one who had the highest passion for Him. And she clung to Him.

Bringing Jesus to Our Mother's House

"I found him whom my soul loves; I held on to him and would not let him go, until I had brought him to my mother's house, and into the room of her who conceived me." You have laid hold of Jesus; you have found fulfillment. But has this seeking of God been only for you? No. For the bride brings Him to the house of her mother, which is the church. She brings Him back to the needy and hurting, to her brothers and sisters.

We all want the Lord, but only the bride will go so far as to find Him and bring Him back to the house. I want to charge you to find Jesus. Do not merely talk about how dead your life or church is—find Him! Pass through your fears. Overcome your passivity and lay hold of Him. The church and our cities need people who are anointed with the presence of Jesus.

You Have Made His Heart Beat Faster

Where was Jesus throughout the time of the bride's searching? Was He aloof, indifferent, sitting in heaven? From the beginning He had been watching, actually longing, for His bride to find Him. He now speaks: "You have made my heart beat faster, my sister, my bride; you have made my heart beat faster with a single glance of your eyes" (4:9).

You are His bride. He is returning from heaven for you! The single glance of your eyes toward Him makes His heart beat faster. Such love is inconceivable. He sees your repentance as your preparation for Him—His bride making herself ready. He beholds you kneeling, weeping at your bedside. He shares your painful longing. He has been watching. And the bridegroom says, "The glance of your eyes has made my heart beat faster."

The Lord has a promise for His bride. He said there will be a fresh and overwhelming baptism of love that will surpass all our knowledge of Him. We will know the height and depth, the width and the breadth of His love. While yet here on earth, we will be filled with His fullness.

We have many tasks, even responsibilities, which have come from heaven. However, the need of our soul is to be with Jesus. The areas of sin in our lives exist simply because we have lived too far from Him. Let us commit our hearts to seeking our God. Let us find Him whom our soul loves and bring Him back to the house of the Lord!

"[That you may really come] to know—practically, through experience for yourselves—the love of Christ, which far surpasses mere knowledge (without experience); that you may be filled (through all your being) unto all the fullness of God—[that is] may have the richest measure of the divine Presence, and become a body wholly filled and flooded with God Himself!" (Eph. 3:19, Amplified).

Lord, even now we lift our eyes toward You. Jesus, grace and truth are realized in You. Grant us grace that the truth of this message will change our lives and compel us in unrelenting love to You! In Jesus' name, amen.

PART TWO

When the Lord Builds the House

Jesus said that nothing was impossible for him who believes.
How is it that we are hemmed in by such little faith,
small prayers and dim vision? God is on our side!
The psalmist said, "Ask of Me, and I will give the nations
as Thine inheritance, and the very ends of the earth as Thy
possession" (2:8). Do not doubt. He has given nations
to His Son before; He shall do it again.

*"I will build My church;
and the gates of hell shall not prevail against it."
Matthew 16:18, KJV*

SEVEN

When the Lord
Builds His House

*I*t is possible for Christ's church to be so properly aligned with heaven that the Holy Spirit actually displaces the powers of darkness over our cities. To the degree that the church is so joined to God, the Lord's presence guards the city: crime and immorality proportionally decline; revival breaks out. But be forewarned: Only if the Lord builds His house will He then guard our cities (Ps. 127:1).

The Corporate, Citywide Church

"And the house, while it was being built, was built of stone prepared at the quarry, and there was neither hammer nor axe nor any iron tool heard in the house while it was being built" (1 Kin. 6:7).

During these past years God has had His church "at the quarry," shaping the leaders, preparing their hearts to become part of the house of the Lord. Under the hammer of the Word, many pastors and lay people have had their rock-hard religious and doctrinal opinions shattered. God has been reducing their definition of Christianity to the biblical proportions of simplicity, purity and devotion to Christ (see 2 Cor. 11:3). At the same time the Lord has also laid His axe to the root system of jealousy and selfish ambition (see James 3:16).

All across the world men and women of God are being fitted together into a living temple for the Lord. Burning in their hearts is a new vision for a united church. Together with their congregations these servants of God are building their churches, not upon the typical American base of self-promotion and human enterprise, but upon a substructure of corporate, citywide prayer and Christian love. With great passion and deep humility, their singular goal is to see Christ Himself formed in the church (see Gal. 4:19). In so doing, they are laying the foundation for the house of the Lord. It is a testimony to Christ's wisdom and power how graciously these "living stones" accept one another and fit together. The Scriptures tell us that when Solomon built the house of the Lord "there was neither hammer nor axe nor any iron tool heard in the house while it was being built" (1 Kin. 6:7).

These men and women, often of very different church backgrounds, are finding themselves kneeling in one another's buildings and praying at each other's side. Their common prayer is that the Almighty might unite them in Christ and finish the house of the Lord—that Christ Himself might heal their cities.

God will answer their prayers. The house of the Lord is beginning to emerge upon the building site of the praying, citywide church. The time of devastation and shaping, of being hammered and cut to size, is nearly over. The day of power is at hand.

The Obedience of Christ

This is not a work born out of compromise. It would be an error to assume the goal of this move of God is unity. No, our objective is obedience. Out of obedience to God in prayer and true desire to be Christlike, a new meaning to unity has come.

Our focus is upon Christ. Paul instructed the church to take "every thought captive to the obedience of Christ" (2 Cor. 10:5). The areas of our thought life which are not captive to Christ are the areas where we are losing our battle against hell. But when our vision is focused upon the Lord and becoming like Him in obedience, the conclusion of what Paul wrote will be fulfilled: "And we are ready to punish all disobedience, whenever your obedience is complete" (2 Cor. 10:6).

It would be presumption to speculate on all that this verse means. We know that Paul was not referring to flesh and blood; he was not warring according to the flesh (see Eph. 6:12). The implication here is that when the obedience of the church is made complete there will be an unleashing of the mightiest display of spiritual power the world has ever seen.

This revelation of power was *not* attained in Paul's day. The provision was there in that the prince of this world was "judged," "rendered powerless" and "disarmed" at the cross, but obviously "all disobedience" was not punished in the first century.

Let us ask the Lord Himself: Is there something yet to come through the obedient church that will bring judgment upon spiritual wickedness and disobedience and also deliver many cities?

When the Lord Guards the City

"Unless the Lord builds the house, they labor in vain who build it; unless the Lord guards the city, the watchman keeps awake in vain" (Ps. 127:1). Before we discuss this verse it is important to explain a characteristic often found in the Hebrew Scriptures. Often the Old Testament writers communicated truth by repeating two views of the same thought. We see this especially in Psalms and Proverbs. An example would be: "With the fruit of a man's mouth his stomach will be satisfied; he will be satisfied with the product of his lips" (Prov. 18:20). The same concept is presented twice in two ways. Another example is: "I will open my mouth in a parable; I will utter dark sayings of old" (Ps. 78:2). Truth is conveyed using a poetic rhythm that is both beautiful and functional—a way of compressing two corresponding thoughts into one idiom.

In this regard, when the psalmist admonishes, "Unless the Lord builds the house, they labor in vain who build it; unless the Lord guards the city, the watchman keeps awake in vain," he is saying the same truth in two ways. The work of the Lord is a bridge connecting these two thoughts: the house He builds will stand; the city He guards will be protected.

How can the Lord guard the city? The house of the Lord is a house of prayer; intercession brings the presence of God into the city. Let me say this another way: *When* the Lord builds the house, *then* the Lord will guard the city. The specifications of His building plans require His people to be praying, loving and investing themselves into their cities, empowered by His anointing. The house of the Lord will change our communities!

Jesus confirms this in His promise that "I will build My church; and the gates of hell shall not prevail against it" (Matt. 16:18, KJV). He is stating that when His house is built in obedience to His Word the strongholds of evil over individuals and cities will be broken.

When there is revival in a city, what happens to the powers of darkness in the heavenly places? Where do they go? They are displaced by the fullness of God's Spirit in the regional church. Paul tells us that it is "through the church" that the manifold wisdom of God is revealed "to the rulers and the authorities in the heavenly places" (Eph. 3:10). And what is happening in the spirit realm? The church is blessed with "every spiritual blessing in the heavenly places in Christ" (Eph. 1:3). The prevailing influence upon society in this case comes from heaven; the Lord guards the city!

When the church is not built according to Christ's directives but remains selfish and divided, the principalities and powers have access in a greater degree to the souls of men. In such cities, spiritual wickedness guards the city.

One does not have to be very discerning to see this is true. On your next drive from the country into a city, you will notice a distinguishable cloud of oppression as you enter the city. That invisible barrier marks the influence of the ruling spirits of the community. The demonic power of that area is the "strong man, fully armed," who "guards his own homestead"; whose "possessions are undisturbed" (Luke 11:21).

But when the church is obedient to Christ, it will be united with other believers and unstoppable by the powers of hell. Through the church—its prayer, love and action—the Lord will guard the city.

Whatever You Bind Will Be Bound

Let me explain the interaction between the spirit world and the thoughts and actions of men. As I see it, the spirit realm can be accessed and occupied by either angels or demons, depending upon the attitude of man. Although the earth is the Lord's, He put all things under man's feet; that is, under man's responsibility.

When Satan told Jesus that all the world and its glory have "been handed over to me" (Luke 4:6), he was speaking a half-truth. The world has indeed been given to the devil, not by God, but by man!

We have wrongly assumed that the devil has divine approval to attack our neighborhoods and cities. Satan has access to the domain of darkness, but he can only occupy those areas where mankind, through sin, has allowed him.

Thus, Jesus tells the church, "whatever you shall bind on earth shall be bound in heaven, and whatever you shall loose on earth shall be loosed in heaven" (Matt. 16:19; 18:18). Notice that Jesus gave the same instruction for two seemingly different situations. The context of Matthew 16:18-19 deals with the devil, while the focus of Matthew 18:15-18 is sin. These realms are interconnected. The sinfulness of mankind, his evil thoughts, words and actions, is the very shelter of the devil over our cities! Since this is true, then righteousness in the church proportionally displaces the devil in the spirit realm, offering Satan no hiding place. He may tempt, but he cannot abide. Indeed, when the church truly draws near to God, the devil flees.

55

A New Vision

If we work together to build the house of the Lord, our strengths will be amplified rather than diminished. One of the pastors in my city has been used by God to picket abortion clinics and stores which sell pornography. Before the churches began to pray together, the most people he ever mustered for a protest was 120. However, because a larger number of churches are united with him now in prayer, over four thousand people came recently to stand against abortion! Since then the local television stations and newspapers have been far more sympathetic to the cause of the unborn.

Where the churches are united, the benefit upon teens will be wonderful. Imagine how it would be if there were a citywide youth group where large numbers of Christian teens could meet and unite. Older teens could develop leadership skills and pastoral care over younger teenagers.

Without limiting their overseas missions, pastors are realizing the first mission field they need to support is local. Ministers in churches are beginning to build together, training individuals from their congregations to go to other churches in the city where together the entire local Christian community is being built up.

Ultimately, how will the house of the Lord differ from current Christianity? Although the Lord has visited the church with revival in the past, He will dwell in power in His house. Healing and deliverance will be commonplace; holiness and grace will fill the atmosphere. Where the house of the Lord is built, the protection of the Lord will be felt.

A Living Testimony

Our ministry is located in Cedar Rapids, Iowa. When we first started praying together with other pastors and intercessors in the city, the state of Iowa was experiencing an 11 percent increase in violent crime. During this same time, however, in Cedar Rapids violent crime *decreased* 17 percent. FBI files confirm that Cedar Rapids became the safest city of over 100,000 people in the United

States in 1988. In spite of the enemy's counterattack, Cedar Rapids remains one of the safest cities in the nation. We continue to experience many wonderful and significant breakthroughs in our city.

To the degree that the Lord's house is established in our cities, lawlessness will proportionally decrease. The time is soon upon us when, unless we are building the Lord's house, our labors may actually be in vain. But the Holy Spirit's encouragement to us is unwavering: When the Lord builds the house, then the Lord will guard the city.

Lord, thank You for Your dealings in my life. Thank You for shaping my heart to fit in with other believers in my city. O God, increase Your work in this region until Your entire church is one body, one force, one weapon in Your hand against evil! Build and then enter Your house, Lord Jesus. Open the door of Your house, and step onto our streets. Guard our cities with power. In Jesus' name, amen.

EIGHT

Forgiveness and the Future of Your City

*T*he redemptive power of God is released when people forgive each other. Individuals, families, churches and even the atmosphere of a city can change when pardon is released. When such a display of grace is poured out, principalities and powers are neutralized often without so much as speaking a word against them.

The Power in Forgiveness

Perhaps nothing so typifies the transforming, cleansing power of God as that which is experienced when a soul receives forgiveness. It is the power of new life, new hopes and new joy. It is the river of life flowing again into the cold, hardened valleys of a once-embittered heart. Forgiveness is at the core and is the essence of revival itself.

Whenever pardon is abundantly given, there is a definite and occasionally dramatic release of life against the powers of death in the heavenly places. Observe the release of life when Jesus, on the cross, prayed, "Father, forgive them" (Luke 23:34). At that very moment every demonic principality and power which had infiltrated man's relationship with God was "disarmed" (Col. 2:15). As the spikes were driven into the palms and feet of the Savior, and as He pleaded "they know not what they do," hell's gates unlocked, tombs opened, the veil into the holy place rent and heaven itself opened—all because of His forgiveness. Even many dead arose (see Matt. 27:51-53). The hand of God shattered boundaries in every known dimension through the power released when Christ forgave our sins.

Jesus, on the cross, "canceled out [our] certificate of debt." By His act of forgiveness He simultaneously disarmed "the rulers and authorities" (Col. 2:14,15). Likewise, when we forgive there is a canceling of debts and a disarming of the enemy. You see, Christ's forgiveness disarmed the devil in mankind's heavenward relationship with God; our pardon of others disarms the enemy in our earthly relationships toward one another.

Consider the last time you experienced full healing in a severed relationship. It is likely that such words as "wonderful" and "glorious" were used to describe the baptism of love that renewed your souls. Can we see that forgiveness is the very heart of Christ's message?

Several years ago I met an Islamic scientist from India. Islam is a religion based on man's righteousness, and he had stumbled over the lack of "good works" among the Christians he knew. As I witnessed to him, I soon found myself in a debate concerning the credibility of Christianity. As our discussion grew mutually more ardent, two of my children approached; one was crying, the other angry.

My procedure in disciplining the children is to have a brief "hearing" in which I judge both sides of the conflict. I discern who is the victim and who is the offender, and I have the victim pass sentence on the offender. I ask, "How many spankings should I give?" The victim knows that next week the roles may be reversed and he or she may be the culprit in need of pardon. Thus the wounded child extends mercy and says, "No spankings." The result is that the kindness of the victim leads the offender to repentance. As the judge, I did not have to punish the guilty because the debt was canceled; the victim's mercy triumphed over judgment. The result is that enmity is broken, children are reconciled, and friendship is restored.

Our "trial" was over quickly, and the children were happy once again. All this had taken place while my Muslim friend watched, and when I turned back to him to continue our debate, he said, "There is no need to continue. I have just seen the power of Christianity!"

One of the most fundamental truths of our faith is that through Christ we have received forgiveness from God for sins, and because of Christ we can forgive one another. Someone pays the price to absorb the offense to themselves, but in so doing they release the power of God, bringing healing to souls. It may rend the heavens, as Christ's forgiveness did for us, or it may rend the heart when we forgive one another. Whether the result is spectacular or subtle, however, forgiveness is the very life of God.

When Stephen forgave his murderers, a plea for mercy with "Saul of Tarsus" written on it ascended to the heart of God. Could it have been the divine response to Stephen's forgiveness that was instrumental in transforming Saul into Paul, an apostle of God?

Consider the reunion of Jacob and Esau. Esau is known in the Scriptures as a hardened man, one who sold his birthright for a single meal. Yet as Jacob bowed seven times to the ground in repentance, asking forgiveness from Esau, a flow of life from the heart of God flooded the embittered Esau. Scripture tells us there was such a release of grace into his soul that he "ran to meet [Jacob] and embraced him, and fell on his neck and kissed him, and they wept" (Gen. 33:1-4). Esau's heart melted, and he chose to forgive the repentant Jacob. So moved was he that he ran and embraced Jacob, kissed him and then wept on his neck. When we truly desire to walk in repentance and reconciliation, even a man as hardened as Esau was can be touched by God!

We see this divine flow of life again when Joseph was reunited with his brothers. Having been sold by them into slavery, Joseph had every right to be bitter. Instead he chose to forgive. Note carefully the washing of the Spirit of God through these lives as Joseph was reconciled with his brothers: "Then Joseph could not control himself....And he wept so loudly that the Egyptians heard it, and the household of Pharaoh heard of it. Then Joseph said to his brothers, 'I am Joseph!' " (Gen. 45:1-3a).

Joseph was so full of love and forgiveness that he actually begged his guilt-laden brothers to forgive themselves. He pleaded, "Do not be grieved or angry with yourselves. For God sent me before you to preserve life...and to keep you alive by a great deliverance" (vv. 5,7b).

There was no bitterness, no revenge, no angry last word which preceded his forgiveness. There was only the foretaste of Christ's own unconditional forgiveness to every self-condemned sinner. Indeed, like Joseph, every time we forgive we too "preserve life." We restore our brethren to wholeness "by a great deliverance."

Release Every Man His Servant

Forgiveness is the very spirit of heaven removing the hiding places of demonic activity from the caverns of the human soul. It is every wrong made right and every evil redeemed for good. The power released in forgiveness is actually a mighty weapon in the war to save our cities.

Jeremiah 34 unveils the impact of wholesale forgiveness upon a city, revealing what might have happened had the Jews obeyed God's call of release. The account speaks of more than the reconciliation of family relationships. It deals with the entire city of Jerusalem as well as all the cities of Judah. It reveals the wonderful wisdom and love of God in His willingness to save His stubborn, sinful people.

The story occurs at a time when the Israelites were hopelessly outnumbered. Seemingly every enemy who could carry a sword had it pointed at their cities. We read that "Nebuchadnezzar king of Babylon and all his army, with all the kingdoms of the earth that were under his dominion and all the peoples, were fighting against Jerusalem and against all its cities" (Jer. 34:1).

Is this not our battle as well? Do we not have our own "king of Babylon" with his hosts set against us (Rev. 17-18)? We see armies of demons led by principalities attacking and almost overrunning city after city. The demonic powers of immorality and rebellion, drugs, rock music and satanism, greed, murder and fear have all but swallowed many of our larger communities. Unless the Lord acts mightily, will we not continue to be overwhelmed by the dimensions of the battle?

Such was the plight of Israel. Yet hidden in the ways of God was a plan, a strategy which would both rout the enemy and heal their cities. The Lord called them to implement the "Year of Remission," which proclaimed complete and generous release to both servants and slaves (see Deut. 15:1-18).

"Then Jeremiah the prophet spoke all these words to Zedekiah king of Judah...that each man should set free his male servant and each man his female servant, a Hebrew man or a Hebrew woman; so that no one should keep them, a Jew his brother, in bondage. And all the officials and all the people obeyed, who had entered into the covenant that each man should set free his male servant and each man his female servant, so that no one should keep them any longer in bondage; they obeyed, and set them free" (Jer. 34:6-10).

It is one thing to have lost at war and thus become the slave of an enemy, but it is quite another to become the slave of your brother. Yet this kind of servitude was a provision of the Mosaic Law. One's indebtedness could enslave him to another.

However, every seven years Jews who were slaves were to be released, and every fiftieth year all their original properties were to be returned. However, in all the years since the law of remission was issued, Israel has never celebrated this Jubilee, and only rarely has an individual released his slaves. Yet at the time Jeremiah spoke this to the king, even with their enemies within striking range the entire nation set about "to free every man his slave."

How does this story relate to us? Whenever any relationship exists outside the shelter of covering love, it degenerates into a system of mutual expectations and unwritten laws to which we all become debtors. As it was under the Law of Moses, so also it is in the context of human relationships: indebtedness enslaves. Obviously we do not enact the master/slave relationship, but our unforgiving opinion of the offender enslaves him, together with his offense, in our memory.

It is a basic principle of life: Where there is no love, of necessity there must be law. And where there is law, there are both debts and debtors. To counter the debilitating effect indebtedness has upon relationships, Jesus commanded His disciples to maintain love among all men. For love transcends the "ledger sheet mentality"; it refuses to take "into account a wrong suffered" (1 Cor. 13).

How shall we deal with debts? Christ warned we would not be forgiven unless we forgave others. Whenever we are unforgiving, we are also reacting. Those un-Christlike reactions to offenses become our sin before God. To be released from our reactions we must return to the cause, the first offense, and be reconciled. As we forgive, we are forgiven and restored; life and balance return to our souls.

In our story from Jeremiah the Judeans did not merely forgive each other, they made a "covenant" before God. They cut a calf in two, and they passed "between its parts" (v. 18). This was the same kind of covenant relationship Abraham had made centuries earlier with the Lord (see Gen. 15:10,17,18). They made a covenant with God to release one another!

The redemptive plan of God was this: If the Israelites set free their slaves, they would not be taken as slaves. If they showed mercy, He would show Himself merciful as well. The destruction of their cities would be averted, for "mercy triumphs over judgment" (James 2:13). Although they were sinners, love would fulfill the law and make all things clean for them (see Gal. 5:14; Luke 11:41).

Look what happened to the Judeans' enemies as the populace enacted the covenant of remission. Something marvelous was occurring in the spirit realm. Supernaturally the Lord drew "the king of Babylon...away" (v. 21). At the very moment the people were being merciful to one another and releasing their slaves, their enemy was drawn away, and their war ended! What they did on earth was actually being done for them in the heavens.

We are just like the Judeans of Jeremiah's day. Our cities are also under attack, and no program or government aid can help us. What we need desperately is divine intervention and deliverance. We need to see the mercy of God and His convicting power poured out supernaturally on the people!

Some may say our cities are like Sodom—beyond saving, beyond redemption. This argument usually arises from a heart whose love has grown weak. Yet the first cause of sin in Sodom was a lack of mercy. He said, "Behold, this was the guilt of your sister Sodom: she and her daughters had arrogance, abundant food, and careless ease, but she did not help the poor and the needy. Thus they were haughty and committed abominations before Me. Therefore I removed them when I saw it" (Ezek. 16:49-50).

This prophecy concerning Sodom came from Ezekiel, who was Jeremiah's contemporary. He was probably speaking to many of the same people who later released their slaves. The root sin, the cause of Sodom's wickedness, was not perversity but selfishness. It was a city full of wealth but without mercy, refusing to help the poor and needy. Thus, they went on to commit abominations before the Lord. Any society that hardens its heart toward mercy opens its heart toward hell. But when a people become merciful, mercy is allotted to them.

The appeal of God is that we return to love and forgiveness. The Israelites, like the Sodomites, had fallen far short of the Lord's standard of righteousness, as we have done also. Yet, for all their sins, God had one more plan, one more divine alternative that might have completely changed the end of the book of Jeremiah and brought lasting deliverance. It was pure, and it was simple. The Lord called for a covenant of forgiveness; His plan was to flood the heavenlies with mercy. The very mercy the Judeans were giving to each other would pave the way for God to show mercy toward them, and it worked: The king of Babylon, his armies and every one of Israel's enemies left the nation!

They Fell From Grace

The Lord gave the Judeans one last opportunity, but when their enemies left and the pressure upon them abated, they did something terrible. Instead of maintaining their mercy, they brought their brothers back into slavery.

"But afterward they turned around and took back the male servants and the female servants, whom they had set free, and brought them into subjection for male servants and for female servants" (Jer. 34:11). Under the fear of death they released their slaves. Now with the threat of death removed, they returned to their selfishness. We need to understand that where there is a decrease of love there will be an increase of demonic activity in our relationships. The Jews released their slaves, and the enemy left. But like so many of us, when the pressure was removed, they returned to their sin: They took back their slaves.

"Therefore thus says the Lord, 'You have not obeyed Me in proclaiming release each man to his brother, and each man to his neighbor. Behold...I will give [you] into the hand of those who seek [your] life, and into the hand of the army of the king of Babylon which has gone away from you. Behold, I am going to command,' declares the Lord, 'and I will bring them back to this city; and they shall fight against it and take it' " (Jer. 34:12-22). The Lord gave them exactly what they gave each other. They made their brethren slaves; their enemies in turn made them slaves. It is ironic that when Israel was finally carried off into Babylon, a number of these very slaves were left in the land. Many of the individuals who had been re-enslaved were assigned the properties of their former masters.

But do not be mistaken. As the book of Lamentations testifies, this was no happy ending. However, for us the final outcome of the war against our cities is yet to be written. There is still time to flood the heavens with the mercies of God. If there is citywide repentance for unforgiveness, even "Esaus" will fall weeping upon the necks of their brothers. If there is a canceling of debts, deliverance can come as it did to Joseph's brothers, even to those who are guilty of betrayal. Wherever love prevails, the strongholds of hell will be torn down, and the spiritual armies surrounding our cities will be disarmed.

This release of divine power is resident even now in our capacity to set one another free from indebtedness. All we must do is forgive our debtors and maintain the attitude of forgiveness. As we release each other, God Himself will begin to release our brethren, our churches and ultimately our cities. It is up to us, as individuals, to flood the spirit realms with mercy. For whatever we loose on earth will be loosed and given back to us in the heavenlies.

Father, we have sinned against You and against our brethren. By our lack of mercy and the hardness of our hearts toward our brethren, we have allowed the devil access to the church and to our cities; we have brought judgment to our land. Forgive us, Lord! In all sincerity we make a covenant of forgiveness with You and all men. We choose, as did Jesus, to absorb the debt unto ourselves and free one another. As we release one another, liberate us from the grip of our enemy. As we show mercy, pour Your mercy upon our cities! In Jesus' name, amen.

NINE

The House
of Prayer

*T*o reach our cities, Christ must reach His church. He must convict our hearts of the arrogance and pride, the jealousy and selfish ambition that have clouded our vision. We must be cleansed of these sins so Jesus can unite us against evil.

Revival Follows Obedience

"And when He approached, He saw the city and wept over it" (Luke 19:41). If Jesus came today and gazed upon His church in its carnality and division, if He probed into our prayerlessness and lack of outreach, would tears flood His eyes over our cities, even as He wept over Jerusalem? I tell you, He would weep over our cities as well.

Even now Christ's hands are extended in love toward our churches and our cities. Knowing we cannot win the citywide war as isolated, individual churches, Jesus longs to bring us together for prayer. He said, "How often I wanted to gather your children together, just as a hen gathers her brood under her wings, and you would not have it!" (Luke 13:34).

Please hear Christ's heart. He said, "How often I wanted to gather your children together!" Time and again He has called us to humble ourselves and in united, heartfelt prayer allow Him to heal our land. But Jesus says, "You would not have it!" The lack of blessing in our cities is not God's fault, nor is it only because of the sins of the world. A number of our national problems are because the church has been caught up in its own agendas and programs. We have disdained Christ's call to obedience and prayer.

Maybe we are waiting for God to do something to unite us. Perhaps we are waiting for revival before we truly obey Him. We must see that revival follows obedience, not obedience after revival.

Indeed, this message is another occasion of Christ's love seeking to gather us together beneath His wings. The question is not, will there be revival? Rather the challenge is, when will we obey Him that revival might come? Our dilemma is not, will the Lord bless His church, but, when will the believing Christians obey their Lord and join together for prayer?

The Hour of Our Visitation

God has a purpose for this country that the enemy wants to stop. Even in the midst of our fallen condition, and while many are warning of impending judgments, the Lord repeats to us what He said to Jerusalem. "If you had known in this day, even you, the things which make for peace" (Luke 19:42). There are things which make for peace, even in our cities and in our generation. When Jesus spoke these words, the Jews were about to be destroyed! But even in the anticipation of coming destruction He said there were things that would turn the city from evil and bring it into peace.

What were those things? We can see them more clearly if we note that immediately after Jesus warned Jerusalem of her fate, He entered the temple and began to cast out those who were selling wares, saying to them, "It is written, 'And My house shall be a house of prayer' ['for all the nations,' Mark 11:17], but you have made it a robber's den" (Luke 19:46).

Jesus rebuked the Jews because they had made His Father's house a house of merchandise. This has little to do with the practice of selling Christian books or tapes in the church building, which is simply a transfer of spiritual information in a nonprofit way. What we have possibly been guilty of is the merchandising of the gospel on a much larger scale. As churches we sometimes merchandise our spiritual gifts: tongues or healing and prophecy. We peddle our evangelism, our children's programs, our youth groups and home fellowships. God gave these differences to enhance us, while Satan uses them to divide us.

It certainly is not wrong to present such programs under the anointing of the Lord. What is wrong is to market our uniqueness as a commodity to lure people from one church to another. Christ said His Father's house would not be a house of merchandise, but a house of prayer. Corporate, heartfelt, citywide prayer for our communities and our nation is the most essential dynamic for seeing our society turned and our cities redeemed.

You say it will take more than prayer. Yes, it will take repentance and humility and, above all else, a return to the Person and words of Jesus. But our cities are not worse than Nineveh. When Nineveh humbled itself, repented and prayed, destruction was averted.

The House of Prayer

You may feel your community is relatively safe, that the oppression upon our land does not concern you. Your optimism is a delusion. Unless there is a buffer of prayer and aggressive Christianity in your town, it will only be a matter of time before it is invaded by the advancing flood of evil.

Jesus is seeking to bring His church to the place where it becomes, literally, a house of prayer. There are already numbers of churches gathering together in many cities for daily prayer. This will continue until there will not be enough room for everyone to pray in only one church. People will be meeting in many places two and three times a day, as it was in the great New York revival of 1857-59. Pastors, church leaders and people from many congregations will be seeking God together.

The Lord will test the endurance of this newly praying church, but gradually the power of God will be released in the cities of prayer. The extraordinary presence of the living Christ will make miracles seem ordinary. Faith will once again rest on the demonstration of the Spirit and not upon the wisdom of man; multitudes will be genuinely saved.

You see, there are things which make for peace. Pastors and their congregations must repent of the independence, spiritual pride and insecurities which have kept them isolated from each other. God has wonderful, awesome plans for our cities. But the substructure of these "things which make for peace" is the citywide church becoming a house of prayer.

Jesus said that any house or city divided against itself shall not stand. It cannot stand. The only way we can stand victorious before our enemies is if we kneel humbly before our Lord together.

Will Your City Become Darkness or Light?

As the return of Christ draws near, God will release a wave of revival that will enable entire cities, and in some cases even nations, to be turned to the Lord. Even now the Soviet Union and Eastern bloc nations are being prepared for a great harvest. If the churches in Africa free themselves from competition and strife, that continent will also experience salvation on a national level.

At the same time there will be many more cities and nations that will not turn to Him. In fact, communities will ally themselves so thoroughly with the powers of evil that a visible darkness, as in Egypt during the exodus, will actually settle upon them (Is. 60:1-3). Even now many large cities in the United States and Europe stand in the balance as to whether or not they will turn toward God or become places of utter darkness, great despair and destruction.

Before we presumptuously judge these cities, however, let us realize again that the deciding factor in God's judgment is not the sin of the world, but sin in the church. Judgment begins first "with the household of God" (1 Pet. 4:17). The direction of each individual city, for the most part, will rest upon the condition of the *church* in that city.

If the church in the city is united, praying together and warring side-by-side against evil, there will be hope for that area. If there is jealousy and selfish ambition in the corporate church, there will be no successful strategies against evil nor barriers against the increase of wickedness. We must understand: *God has placed the responsibility for our cities upon our shoulders!*

We suggest that, if you are a pastor, you contact other pastors in your city to organize corporate congregational prayer at least once a week. If you are an intercessor, we encourage you to gather other intercessors and begin praying for the healing of the church and the beginning of the house of prayer. In our conferences our policy is to initiate a minimum of five or as many as twenty different church sites throughout a city where people from various congregations can gather together and pray. For more information about starting a citywide prayer group or becoming part of an existing one, please write to Advancing Church Ministries, P.O. Box 10102, Cedar Rapids, IA 52410.

TEN

Fighting for the Nation and the Church

G od can overcome evil in either of two ways. He can eradicate wickedness with destructive judgments, as in the case of Sodom and Gomorrah, or He can overcome evil with good. When the Lord determines to act in the way of destructive judgments, it is as a last resort. The Father's first choice is always to move in mercy. In the heart of God, "mercy triumphs over judgment" (James 2:13).

Mercy Triumphs Over Judgment

"Do not be overcome by evil, but overcome evil with good" (Rom. 12:21). Evil can be overcome with good, but to do so God must use the church. Since the very nature of God is love, redemptive mercy is the ultimate motive behind all His actions. If we will truly please

God, this must become our motive as well.

" 'Do I have any pleasure in the death of the wicked,' declares the Lord God, 'rather than that he should turn from his ways and live?' " (Ezek. 18:23). During many of the natural disasters of recent years, it is obvious that even in the most severe judgments the mercy of God was revealed in miraculous ways. Although calamities will become more devastating before the return of Christ, we must be assured of this: Even in His wrath God is always remembering mercy (see Hab. 3:2).

The first choice of God, however, is to bring mercy *before* destructive judgments fall. His vehicle of mercy is the body of Christ. It is with this motive in His mind that God desires to build the house of the Lord. The righteousness and sanctification that the living, holy church produces in a society can literally preserve that society from much of the evil which might otherwise destroy it.

If we do not rise to this hour, terrible consequences are inevitable. Far more than our worst fears will be realized. We cannot imagine what life will be like when plagues come and bands of lawless, starving individuals rampage through cities, destroying whatever remains of stability. I am not an alarmist, but multitudes are experiencing the beginnings of these things even now in our large inner cities. The breakdown of law and order is already at hand. Many districts have become war zones. There is only one answer, and that is the church. We are at war, and to win this war we must be united.

Those Who Know Their God

In Matthew 24 Jesus speaks of the last days. So terrible is this period that He warns, "Unless those days had been cut short, no life would have been saved." The seriousness of this final hour is a dividing line which finds Christians encamped on either side: some believing in a pre-tribulation rapture and others leaning toward a post-tribulation rapture. After listening to arguments on both sides and seeing the validity and stubbornness of many in both camps, my conclusion is that I am not preparing for *what* is going to happen but *who.* The bride is not making herself ready for a "date," but a marriage. If we are fully given to knowing Christ intimately, not only will we enjoy His presence, but we will gain spiritual strength for whatever the future holds!

The key, therefore, to living victoriously in the last days is not knowing timetables, but knowing God. Daniel foretold that, in the midst of worldwide distress, those who "know their God will display strength and take action" (Dan. 11:32). From a position of knowing the heart and nature of God, in the midst of great difficulties we will "display strength and take action."

When we consider the wrath of God, it is right that destructive images come to our minds, for such must come upon the whole world. However, Isaiah 61 gives us clear insight into the purpose of "the day of vengeance of our God." It is to "comfort all who mourn, to grant those who mourn in Zion, giving them a garland instead of ashes...the mantle of praise instead of a spirit of fainting" (vv. 2,3).

The first phase of God's "vengeance" upon the world is aimed at releasing His elect from oppression. But God does not stop there. His grace continues. Taking these very individuals who were fainting under their enemies' oppression, He raises them up to spiritual maturity. "So they will be called oaks of righteousness, the planting of the Lord, that He may be glorified" (v. 3).

You see, as God's anger is released against His enemies, there will be great deliverance among all His people simultaneously. Indeed, where they have suffered most from personal defeat, in those very areas they will walk in victory. Ultimately these oaks of righteousness will advance the very power of redemption, which God applied to their hearts, to the cities around them. "Then they will rebuild the ancient ruins, they will raise up the former devastations, and they will repair the ruined cities, the desolations of many generations" (v. 4).

For everyone who shares a true yearning for the righteousness of God, and for each soul that earnestly desires to be like Jesus, the day of God's vengeance is your hour of fulfillment! As we watch the spiritual collapse of oppression in the communist nations, can it be that we are actually living in the first stages of the vengeance of God?

Are we in a time of anointed release of the church to see the "ancient ruins" of God's house rebuilt and the "ruined cities," the "desolations of many generations," repaired?

Whether this is that unique time or not remains to be seen, but I would like to remind you that in difficult times the church has consistently been God's tool to bring healing to the nations. Whether it was with William Booth or John and Charles Wesley in England, Martin Luther in Germany or Francis of Assisi in Italy, it has always been *through the elect* that the Lord has impacted and transformed society. The issue need not even be end-time events; *today* the need is great enough to call the elect of God to "display strength and take action."

Who are the elect? The elect have been, at various times, Jews, Romans, Germans, Englishmen, Americans, Chinese—persons of any nationality who heard the heart of God, overcame the unbelief and discouragement of those around them, and literally moved their world toward heaven.

Remember this: The Lord's first choice is always to extend mercy to our cities and turn them from the path of ruin; mercy triumphs over judgment. To do so He needs us. The answer to the present condition in our nation is not new government programs or new policies, but New Testament Christianity—oaks of righteousness that are empowered with the redemptive mercy of God.

ELEVEN

Even
Sodom

*G*od does not hinder the healing of our land. Rather our apathy and unbelief keep us from grasping the potential offered to us in the gospel of Christ. Do not marvel that entire cities can be saved. The Scripture tells us that nations will come to our light and kings to the brightness of our rising (see Is. 60:1-3).

All We Lack Is Christlikeness

"He then began to reproach the cities in which most of His miracles were done, because they did not repent" (Matt. 11:20). Jesus has a word to say, not only to us as individuals, but to entire cities as well. In anger He rebuked Chorazin, Bethsaida and Capernaum (see Matt. 11:21); with tears He cried out to Jerusalem (see

Luke 13:34). Yes, Jesus spoke to entire cities and expected them to repent, and He expects cities today to repent as well. The scale is different, but the grace to change is the same. Yes, Christ's message sounds a trumpet loud enough for whole cities to hear and be turned.

It was in this very context of reproving communities, however, that Jesus made a statement which unveiled God's redemptive power that is waiting and available for even the most wicked of cities. Listen to His rebuke and its hidden promise. He said, "For if the miracles had occurred in Tyre and Sidon which occurred in you, they would have repented long ago in sackcloth and ashes" (Matt. 11:21).

Jesus said that His life, revealed in power, can bring even the vilest of cities, places which ought to be destroyed, to "sackcloth and ashes." The strategy, therefore, to win our cities is for the church to reveal Christ's life in power. Yes, the revelation of Christ in us as individuals, and the power of Christ displayed corporately through us, can turn our worst cities back toward God!

Today many cities are ripe for revival. What hinders the turning of the people's hearts? The answer lies with the church, with our sins of self-righteousness, apathy and unbelief. The Lord said, "If My people humble themselves and pray...I will heal their land." Whether or not we actually attain Christ's level of faith, God "desires...all men to be saved" (1 Tim. 2:4). With this in mind, Paul taught that entreaties and prayers should be made on behalf of all men, "for kings and all who are in authority" (1 Tim. 2:1-4). The sacrifice of Christ provides for the salvation of all men, and since the Father Himself desires all men to be saved, heaven waits only for the church to act.

One may say, But that was then. Our cities are worse now. They are beyond redemption. Not so. Jesus continued His rebuke of cities by saying, "If the miracles had occurred in Sodom which occurred in you, it would have remained to this day" (Matt. 11:23). Amazingly, Jesus said even Sodom could find repentance!

I have heard many ministers compare Los Angeles or New York to Sodom. Fine. But these cities have seen hell, so now let the church show them heaven. They need to see Jesus revealed in His church. The promise of Christ is that even Sodom could repent in the atmosphere and revelation of Christ's power. If there is hope for Sodom, there is hope for your city as well.

The Obstruction to Revival: Complacency

When we picture cities, we tend to see skylines and factories, streets and schools. Jesus, however, sees people. He beholds husbands arguing with wives while their children tremble in fear. He sees drugs being sold on playgrounds and teenagers having abortions. He suffers at the bedside of the hospitalized and the shut-ins. The heart of Christ grieves with the loneliness of the elderly and identifies with the struggle of the handicapped.

Yes, the eyes of the Lord probe the spirit and humanity of the city. From His eternal perspective He also beholds the most terrible event known to man. He sees the overwhelming horror, the utter despair an unsaved soul experiences as he realizes he is, indeed, dead and going to hell. And, in the midst of it all, He sees the church—His church, purchased at the cost of His own precious blood—sitting comfortably, remote control in hand, watching television.

Jesus does not have a problem with the hot or cold dimensions of life. It is the lukewarm that He will spew from His mouth (see Rev. 3:15-16). What stopped the cities of Chorazin, Bethsaida and Capernaum—communities which already had the blessing of Christ's healing—from embracing ongoing renewal? They assumed Christ's love was given only to enrich them. All they saw were the rewards of Christ without understanding His requirements.

The church today is so similar in attitude to those ancient cities that it is frightening. The majority of the first-century saints gave their lives to Christ with the full knowledge that they would face persecution, suffering and possibly death for their faith. Such was the character and vision of the church in the first century.

The main emphasis of much of our Christianity, however, is to help believers become "normal." So much of our contemporary teaching keeps alive the very nature Jesus calls us to crucify. We need to re-evaluate our preaching. Are we preaching the cross and the call to follow Jesus? What are we training our people to become?

Please hear me; the Father's goal is not merely to bless us but to transform us into the image of His Son. He desires to use us to turn our cities back to Him. But God has made no provision for the healing of our land apart from our becoming Christlike. Once we realize this vital truth, we shall return to the source of New Testament Christianity, and our cities will have hope for redemption. When the church demonstrates the love and power of Christ, repentance and revival can occur even in a place like Sodom.

Kingdom-Conquering Faith

Often I have heard Christians presumptuously state what they were "going to do to the devil." The outcome, however, has often been a testimony of what the devil did to them. At one time or another we have all fallen into boasting of our plans or achievements only to fall headlong, tripped by our own pride. Consequently, it is vital to recognize the pitfalls of presumptuous or arrogant "faith" before we approach our cities.

Nevertheless, while we want to avoid the excesses of presumption, the consequences of unbelief are worse. Jesus never rebuked anyone, saying, "O ye of too much faith." We have suffered because we have been too weak to believe God's promises. There is a legitimate dimension of faith that is coming from God. It is motivated by love and guided by wisdom, and it is coming from heaven to capture our cities. It is no less powerful than the faith of those who "turned the world upside down" in the first century.

Abraham exercised this same faith in respect to the promise of God. Not wavering in unbelief, he grew strong in faith. He knew the heart of God and that it is the Lord's very nature to give "life to the dead" and call "into being that which does not exist" (Rom. 4:17). Abraham knew that if the Lord had but ten righteous men He could deliver Sodom! God is giving us this kind of faith for our cities.

Look at the achievements of our forefathers in faith. Remember, these individuals served God in the Old Testament. God has given greater promises to us (Heb. 11:39).

Through faith God's people "conquered kingdoms, performed acts of righteousness, obtained promises, shut the mouths of lions, quenched the power of fire, escaped the edge of the sword, from weakness were made strong, became mighty in war, put foreign armies to flight" (Heb. 11:33-34).

Many Christians think knowing the promises is the same as obtaining them. True faith literally *obtains* the promises of God. Faith "conquered kingdoms"; faith can conquer our cities! It can draw Christ's very righteousness into the church, enabling us to lay down our lives for our communities as He did for the world.

Our flesh says, I am weak. Yes, but weakness is an improvement over all who are strong in their own strength. Through faith, which works through grace, we grow from "weakness," and in Christ we are "made strong." Faith "shuts the mouths of lions"—those voices which would otherwise devour us with discouragement or fear. Because of Christ's accomplished victory, and through the knowledge of His Word, we are learning to become "mighty in war." We know that, if evil can enter our cities through our negligence, evil can leave through our diligence. Indeed, it is possible to put the "foreign armies" of hell "to flight."

We might ask, But does this fit into my eschatology? Our "eschatologies" can be an excuse for unbelief. The fact is that we do not know when Jesus is returning. What we do know is that the devil is here now and has invaded our cities.

Where is the church? The body of Christ has been trapped in a doctrine which says: between now and when Jesus returns, only apostasy and more evil will exist. Paul warned about this time, saying, "In the later times some will fall away from the faith" (1 Tim. 4:1).

We must incorporate into our understanding the historic fact of the Dark Ages; for over one thousand years the church was in unbelievable sin and apostasy. It is quite possible that the major part of the falling away has already occurred. We may actually be in what the Bible refers to as the "periods of restoration" (Acts 3:24).

Paul said that in later times "some" will fall away. He did not say "all," but "some." From what will they fall away? They will fall away from the faith! Let us become personal in this matter of the apostasy. Let us not look for the apostasy anywhere else but in the areas of our own hearts. Where have *you* fallen from *confident, expectant faith?* Where are *you* imprisoned by unbelief? If you look at your soul and see no hope for Christ to dwell there, to that degree your faith has fallen. Again, if you gaze at the church and see it as irreparably trapped in sin, you have fallen from faith in that area. And if you look at your city and it seems incurable, it is likely that your faith is less than what God has provided.

Apostasy is indeed here, and those who see only a great falling away in the church's future are, in their own way, living in a state of unbelief. They know what God has done, but they are dead to what He is doing. They are blind to the harvest, deaf to the outpouring of the Spirit and ignorant of the emerging, unified church. And if you are such a one, please do not feel condemned, for the grace of God is here to rescue you from the stronghold of unbelief.

Yes, there is terrible darkness in the earth and a gross darkness upon the peoples; severe judgments are here, and they will get worse. However, the promise of God—no, the *command* of God—to His people is full of both faith and power. In the midst of the most terrible of times, the greatest darkness, the Lord proclaims, "Arise, shine; for your light has come, and the glory of the Lord has risen upon you. For behold, darkness will cover the earth, and deep darkness the peoples; but the Lord will rise upon you, and His glory will appear upon you. And nations will come to your light and kings to the brightness of your rising" (Is. 60:1-3). In the midst of the deepest darkness God is sending the brightest light.

If we remain trapped in fear and unbelief, we are already a part of the "falling away from the faith." But if we are cleansing our hearts from sin, if we are uniting our hearts with that holy army being raised up in this hour, God will use us to bring nations to the light of the Lord. Kings will come to the knowledge of the Redeemer. Yes, there is hope even for Sodom to be turned back to God!

Dear Lord, we repent of our unbelief and apathy. Your grace saved us, and we know You can do anything. Give us faith—Your faith—for our cities. Help us see the expanse of Your love and its capacity to turn even a Sodom back to You! In Jesus' name, amen.

TWELVE

The Wings of the Eagle

*W*hat we present in this chapter is not a doctrine that categorically denies any interpretation other than our own. We are using a text by way of application, leaving room for humility, which freely admits there may be other views. At the same time we are establishing grace for faith to work, because our view concerning America may indeed be the mind of Christ.

The Revelation of Jesus

The book of Revelation is, as its first sentence proclaims, the "revelation of Jesus Christ." The book begins with a staggering unveiling of the Lord Jesus in which John is like a dead man before Christ. In chapters 2 and 3 we see Jesus correcting and encouraging

His church; in chapter 4 He is displayed as King upon His throne. In the next segment we behold the Lamb opening the seals of judgment, treading the winepress of God's wrath. And in the final section Christ is revealed in a glory so expansive and brilliant that the earth and sky are swallowed up in light, and in the holy city the sun itself pales and is no more.

Throughout the book Jesus is shown as the eternal commander of the heavenly host, leading a triumphant church into His victory. If we do not see the revelation of Jesus in this book, we will assume it is merely a prophecy of events. Without a vision of Christ, our fears will merely magnify the judgments of God; we will miss the eternal champion who has written His biography before it happens.

The Glorious, Persecuted Church

It is with the reassuring knowledge that Christ has prepared a means of glory and triumph for His church that we proceed into the twelfth chapter of the book of Revelation. So many interpretations of this chapter exist that it is with a sense of trepidation that we attempt to navigate this stormy sea of human opinion.

"And a great sign appeared in heaven: a woman clothed with the sun, and the moon under her feet, and on her head a crown of twelve stars" (Rev. 12:1). Various Bible scholars identify the "woman" in this text as the "Jews," the "church," the *overcoming* church" or the "combined saints of every generation and both covenants." What we know is that this "woman" is "clothed with the sun," which speaks of mature and radiant holiness. We know also that she has the "moon under her feet," which tells us that she treads upon the power of night. She also has on her head a "crown of twelve stars" (Rev. 12:1), which is a symbol of apostolic authority and power.

For the sake of our application and under the shelter of grace, let us say that the "woman" in this verse represents the glorious, mature, overcoming church and her "agony to give birth" (v. 2) symbolizes the highest, most perfect prayers she can utter. What we understand about this passage is that the woman's ministry "births" something that triggers a war in the heavenly places and marks the beginning of the end of Satan's influence on the earth.

The Scripture tells us that the devil, knowing his time is short, will rage against the woman. To protect her, "the two wings of the great eagle were given to the woman" (Rev. 12:14).

What is the great eagle? Could this verse be a prophetic reference to the United States? Since everything in the book of Revelation requires revelation to understand, let us acknowledge with cautious but visionary faith: *The great eagle is the symbol of our country!*

Looking at the Nation God Desires

We cannot ignore the fact that there is great spiritual wickedness in high places over our nation. Yet we would be in just as much error to ignore God's original intention for America which yet remains in His heart. To exercise true discernment, whether it is in regard to a person, a city or a nation, we must look beyond what is obvious to perceive the ultimate call and purpose of God. As Jesus perceived the woman at the well (John 4:1-15), so we must look beyond the harlotry of our country into the call and purposes of God.

"The two wings of the great eagle were given to the woman" (Rev. 12:14). For some the mere suggestion that the United States may be the (or a) fulfillment to this verse resurrects all the negative conclusions they have had about America. I know I run the risk of alienating them against everything else we might present. So let me state plainly: We are not blind patriots or zealous, right-wing conservatives. We see the spirit of Babylon flaunting itself in America's lust for comfort. We have personally warred throughout this country in citywide warfare conferences against the principalities of antichrist, Jezebel and racism. We are by no means ignorant of Satan's devices.

Although the *spirit* of Babylon is upon this land, this nation is *not* the Babylon spoken of in Revelation 17 and 18. The blood of the prophets and the saints has not been poured out upon our streets. In fact, historically, the opposite has been true of the United States: It has been a place of refuge and safety to a persecuted church.

We may argue about the future, but we cannot deny the past. Regardless of where you stand concerning America and its prophetic relationship to this verse, the United States has always been a strong and high tower to the oppressed of the earth. Time and again the wings of this "great eagle" have been given to Christians fleeing persecution in Hungary, England, Germany, Italy and wherever the church was threatened by the dragon.

Despite all the flaws, prejudices and injustices committed by Americans, there simply has never been a nation whose spirit and laws were *more* given to protecting the church than the United States. Can any one nation better fit the prophetic profile of this verse?

The Mystery of America

As we have had to navigate around those who are critical of America, so now we must circumvent the thinking that America was (or is) a Christian country. The United States has been Christianized by the *influence* of Christians, but legally speaking this nation is democratic, not Christian. Because of our religious freedoms, godly men and women evangelized America so that at times Christ Himself touched the soul of the nation. However, America's gift to the world was not Christianity but political freedom.

At its birth in 1776, in a world ruled by tyrants and kings, the United States stood alone as the citadel of freedom. The underlying emphasis in the Bill of Rights is "liberty and justice for all." Its purpose was not to spread Christianity, but to provide a place of freedom where Christianity or any other religion could be spread.

It is a fact that a number of the nation's forefathers were, indeed, Christian. And it is also obvious that they never intended the kind of separation of church and state that is now upon our land. But our forefathers were personally familiar with the governmental oppression levied upon Christians by the churches in Europe. Their goals were to insure freedom so that no one group of people oppressed another and to protect the individual rights of all men.

While we *are* a strong nation, our forefathers chose the "great eagle" as our national emblem not as a symbol of strength but of freedom. Freedom is a "container" in which debate, dissent—even godlessness—can exist. As Thomas Jefferson said, "Freedom of

religion, freedom of the press, and freedom of person...are principles that have guided our steps through revolution and reformation.''
The focus of our forefathers was freedom in all its social forms.

What America has provided for every man is not Christianity but
opportunity. We must do the rest. In our free society the battle is
ideological and spiritual—and relentless, because the same freedoms afforded us are given to our enemies. We have but to relax our
effort and, as we have seen, wickedness prospers.

Our battle must be won and its victory sustained by the truth of
our message and the love and power of our way of life. We must
inspire our society toward Christ rather than attempt merely to
control the people with law.

We must understand this: The very same laws which protect our
right to assemble and worship protect humanists and atheists as well.
Yet we should not fear this arena of battle. Indeed, we enjoy the
greatest advantage, for our message of salvation is more liberating,
more worthy and more relative to mankind's needs than all that the
world offers. But we must *live* the gospel to win our war.

Over the past thirty years we have seen Satan assault this nation
relentlessly. He seized the initiative; he capitalized on America's
freedoms and engaged himself in long-term strategies. While attacking the conscience and imagination of America, the enemy simultaneously attacked a number of the more visible church leaders to
undermine the credibility of the gospel.

To win this war we must not react carnally to what Satan has done.
*We must understand emphatically that we are not warring against
the United States, but the spirits of darkness which have attacked
this country.* The next generation of church leaders must be steadfast
and unwavering in vision. Yes, we can find fault with the nation, but
if that is all we do, we will lose the battle without fighting it.

We must see beyond blind patriotism and the critical ''Jonah
ministry'' into the spiritual realm where the real battle lies. The angel
who came in answer to Daniel's fasting and prayer had to fight to
reach him, having been withstood by the ''prince'' over Persia. This
angel then makes an enlightening statement. He says, ''And in the
first year of Darius the Mede I arose to be an encouragement and a

89

protection for him" (Dan. 11:1). God sent an angel to be an encouragement and a protection to a Persian king! Darius ultimately was responsible for seeing the Jews finish the temple in Jerusalem.

The Lord is building a temple in this country as well, and we need to arise and be an encouragement and protection through prayer to the leaders of our nation. Knowing God's plan, let us give ourselves to the work of redemption, accepting the possibility that the Lord wants to use the United States as a place of protection during some of the difficult days ahead. The Scripture does say the wings of the great eagle *were given* to the woman.

God's Answer for America

We must do all we can for our nation and do so on every front possible. For example, I stand against abortion and pornography. My children and I have picketed abortion clinics and have been arrested. But simply stopping abortion will not stop immorality, which is the *source* of the slaughter of innocents. Our answer must go beyond laws into a divine awakening of our society.

The Christian's battleground does indeed, at times, expand into the courts. But the real war zone is in the spirit and soul of our neighborhoods and cities. As Christians we must take the battle into the same arena in which it has been fought since the first century: prayer and witnessing for Jesus.

Therefore, the plan for healing our nation is the transformation of the church. When *Jesus* is lifted up—not doctrines, programs and buildings, but Jesus—men are drawn unto Him, and society changes.

I do not believe the warnings of America's destruction are irreversible. God has a plan that will bring our nation back to Himself, city by city, church by church, person by person.

Lord, we want to see this nation as You see it. Forgive us for being critical. Forgive us also for blind patriotism. Lord, only You can turn this nation around, but we believe You can do it! Almighty God, empower us to this task, and grant that the wings of the great eagle might be given to the church. In Jesus' name, amen.

PART THREE

The Anointing to Build

Our Father is the Creator.
The Holy Spirit is the Helper.
Jesus is the Word.
If we will simply obey what Jesus says,
the Holy Spirit will help us,
and the Father will establish us as His living house.

"Be strong and courageous and get to work.
Don't be frightened by the size of the task,
for the Lord my God is with you;
he will not forsake you.
He will see to it that everything is finished correctly."
1 Chronicles 28:20, LB

THIRTEEN

The Anointing
to Build

*W*orking with the Holy Spirit, citywide church leaders are receiving the Lord's concern for the entire living church in their regions. To the degree they are building one body of Christ in their cities, they are under the apostolic anointing.

Before we proceed further into this section, there are certain apprehensions we want to defuse. The first is that some may think our goal is to build a new denominational structure. This is completely untrue. The zeal which consumes us and the love which compels us is for our Father's house. Our goal, which we believe is God's goal, is to see the born-again church united under the blood of Christ.

It is our perception that the Lord does not want to eliminate denominational relationships nor separate congregations from the heritage of their forefathers. The Lord does not want to eliminate what we each have received, but to integrate it that light may be given "to all who are in the house" (Matt. 5:15). We believe God's purpose is not to break off national affiliations, but to heal and establish relationships locally.

We also want to remove any sense of human pressure concerning citywide prayer. The desire to pray with other pastors and churches is a gift which God Himself works into the individual. To pluck this fruit prematurely is to have a crop that is both bitter and hard. Those who embrace citywide prayer should do so because of revelation born of God. To seek to motivate pastors by pressure or manipulation will only breed resentment among them; they will fail to find the sweet pleasure which comes when leaders willingly seek God together. If you are concerned about your pastor, pressure heaven with prayer and then leave this work of grace in the Creator's hands.

To those who are not yet involved, let me assure you: The nature of the born-again, praying church is to appeal to God for you and the rest of the body of Christ. Anyone who exudes an attitude of superiority does not represent our hearts nor the heart of God. In truth, our focus is not on becoming leaders, but followers of Jesus; not on a new doctrine, but on obedience to the directives of Christ. We consider all elitism to be arrogant and an attitude God resists. Religious pride was the first stronghold to fall, enabling us, as pastors from different streams, to flow together. God help us that it not be the first sin to arise in this new stirring of His Spirit!

Our prayer is that this section will help initiate a new and holy beginning of the house of the Lord in your city. Let us also note that if a church recognizes Jesus as Lord and the need to be spiritually reborn; if they hold to the truth of the Scriptures and long for the personal return of the Lord Jesus, then we receive them as our brethren. We recognize that Jesus is not only the way to the Father; He is also the bridge to one another. We present to you no other plan or organization than Christ Himself.

94

The Apostolic Anointing

The first-century apostles left us more than their words; they also left us their anointing through which we can build the house of the Lord. As we submit to their instructions, and as we are built upon Christ the cornerstone, grace is being granted to build the living house of the Lord.

What is this apostolic anointing? In the same way a pastor is anointed to care unselfishly for his local congregation, so the apostolic anointing awakens local ministers and intercessors to work together in meeting the needs of the citywide body of Christ. It is a love-motivated awareness that the church is *one*, and when one member suffers we all suffer. We each bear a responsibility for our corporate condition.

However, when we speak of an apostolic anointing, we are not referring to men who are twentieth-century apostles. We have one who is our apostle: Christ, "the apostle and high priest of our confession" (Heb. 2:1). Although invisible, it is He who is guiding, building and setting in order His church. He is with us, even to the end of the age. When we speak of this anointing, we are speaking of a grace coming from Christ the apostle which is settling upon obedient leaders in local Christian churches. Out of His fullness these individuals are beginning to build with apostolic vision.

And what is apostolic vision? "There is one body and one Spirit, just as also you were called in one hope of your calling; one Lord, one faith, one baptism, one God and Father of all who is over all and through all and in all" (Eph. 4:4-6).

Maintaining Freedom

Those anointed with this fresh oil appreciate and respect the diversity of ministry which is already resident in the leaders of the praying, citywide church. They recognize that God has been working in their lives, teaching and guiding, for a number of years. They also recognize that they have received from God an eagerness to pray for and with other pastors and are products of the grace of God, who

95

Himself has brought them to a place of usefulness in building the citywide church.

In the next chapter we will speak of the priority to build using Jesus as the model for the church. But there are other priorities we must embrace if we will see the body of Christ healed. Our uniting with other churches must be free of subtle desires for control. In spite of the problem of sin in the ministry, we should beware of setting up a premature or legalistic standard of accountability, lest we cut off the flow of grace to our work.

This first stage is *relational*, where we are more concerned with our brethren's needs than their creeds. Of course, if an individual is practicing obvious sin or teaching blatant heresy, he should be approached according to the Lord's instructions in Matthew 18:15-18. However, our focus is not upon where we have come from, but upon where and toward whom we are going. After love and friendship are established, correction, in many cases, will take care of itself.

Many in the past have tried to unite the church through governmental or doctrinal conformity. Yet they have failed simply because knowledge instead of the Lord Jesus Christ was the centerpiece of their approach. Consequently, even their desire for unity became divisive, for only those of like standards eventually clustered together. At this point, let us maintain the standards we each have received from God without putting any burden other than love upon one another.

"Now the Lord is the Spirit; and where the Spirit of the Lord is, there is liberty" (2 Cor. 3:17). I am listing liberty as a vital priority because our spiritual freedom is an evidence of the presence and involvement of the Lord. "It was for freedom that Christ set us free; therefore keep standing firm and do not be subject again to a yoke of slavery" (Gal. 5:1). Without freedom to maintain differing doctrinal views or procedures, we will only be exchanging an old form of slavery for a new one.

There will be great variety and power released as individuals with contrasting gifts begin to flow together. In Acts 13:1-2 we read of "prophets and teachers" who were "ministering to the Lord and fasting." Not out of corporate board meetings, but out of corporate prayer and dependency upon the Lord come divine directives for the church: "the Holy Spirit said, 'Set apart for Me Barnabas and Saul' " (v. 2).

Organization is necessary. In fact, "administrations" is one of the ministry gifts mentioned by Paul in 1 Corinthians 12:28. However, God has appointed in the church "first apostles, second prophets, third teachers." There is an order through which administrations function properly. But the organizers must be willing to stay flexible and submissive to the leading of God's anointing.

We all appreciate good administrators who have streamlined operations and facilitated the success of our projects. But if a choice is to be made, it would be better to have leaders who are somewhat disheveled, yet who have hearts passionately addicted to loving God, than administrators who rely only upon human wisdom. They must serve for the sake of communication, not control. They should coordinate ministries of mercy, connecting the hurting with the helping. But they must not be allowed to lead the movement of the city-church independently; that direction must come from the Lord Himself.

Characteristics of Leadership

There are three attitudes of heart that are essential for walking in leadership. The first is our passion for the words of Christ, to which we are devoting the entire next chapter. Without this singular goal, every step we take will be off center and contain a certain element of deception in it.

The second attitude leadership must possess is humility. The Lord tells us through Isaiah, "Heaven is My throne, and the earth is My footstool. Where then is a house you could build for Me? And where is a place that I may rest?" (Is. 66:1). Humility tells us that no amount of our ingenuity, manipulation or money could build a house for the Creator. Whatever we build for Him has a measure of idolatry in it; we ultimately find ourselves worshipping the works of our hands.

However, the Lord *is* speaking here of His house; and He is giving us a clear direction into its nature. He says, "But to this one I will look, to him who is humble and contrite of spirit, and who trembles at My word" (v. 2). Brokenness, a repentant heart and a holy, trembling fear of God are the building materials of the house of the Lord. It is the Lord's building, a place where He can rest.

Apostolic Prayer

The third attitude of anointed leadership is prayer. While we are indeed seeking to see our cities renewed, the kingdom of God is not a social program. It is only as Christ Himself is established in the church that the city can be divinely impacted. When He is lifted up, men are drawn to Him.

Therefore, the thrust of much of our prayer is toward Christ and fellowship with Him. The essence of prayer is a yearning for Jesus. It would be in keeping with the highest purposes of God that entire prayer meetings be devoted to seeking the Lord. Covet such times, for with them the Lord is well-pleased.

Apostolic prayer can also be called "birthing prayer." Paul taught, "My children, with whom I am again in labor until Christ is formed in you" (Gal. 4:19). There are dimensions in the ministry of the church that will not come forth until intercessors pray in the power of this apostolic birthing of the church.

Those under this anointing will be so inflamed with a passion for justice that the Lord will lead them into extended periods of fasting and prayer. An anointed few will even be graced to fast publicly for their region. Many cities will be brought to deep repentance. In some cases not only will abortion be outlawed, but even the cause of abortions (illegitimate pregnancies) will begin to cease. The promise of the Lord is, "Blessed are those who hunger and thirst for righteousness, for they shall be satisfied" (Matt. 5:4).

Apostolic intercession also assumes a posture of spiritual responsibility to support and protect what is newly born and vulnerable. It does not judge the standards of the prayer group but prays for increase in maturity. It is committed to be an example of spiritual maturity in that process.

As this ministry grows there will be those upon whose "prayer shoulders" God places the burden for their cities. They will not and cannot sleep without praying for their communities. They assume a place of responsibility for the condition of the region. They will see a direct correlation between personal prayer and the retreat of the enemy from their cities.

One may question such an office; however, it is not unlike the ministry Martin Luther carried in Germany. He said, "If I miss prayer one day, I feel it; if I fail to pray two days, the entire church feels it; should I not pray three days, all Germany suffers."

The Lord is raising up ministers who are spiritually responsible for their churches and their cities. They will not let a day pass without intercession. When they are in battle, they discern the wider range of assault. This is simply a dimension of the apostolic anointing, the gift of spiritual responsibility in prayer.

Dear Lord Jesus, it is our desire to see Your house built. Yet we acknowledge that heaven is Your throne and earth Your footstool; no house we build is worthy or capable of receiving You. Nevertheless, You have promised to build with humble, contrite people who tremble when You speak. Lord, help us maintain freedom and grace. Help us yield to Your ability to make us a dwelling place of prayer. By Your grace we take responsibility for our churches and our cities. Amen.

FOURTEEN

The Stone the Builders Rejected

*T*he goal of God in this new anointing is to return the church to the simplicity and purity of devotion to Christ. The correct foundation is not just what Jesus did in redemption, but what He commands as Lord. Once the foundation is properly laid within us, the house of the Lord can be built.

Becoming Wise Master Builders

Paul said, "As a wise master builder I laid a foundation" (1 Cor. 3:10). The eternal foundation of the church is the Lord Jesus Christ; we rest and build upon Him. It is wisdom to build the Lord's house with only Jesus in mind, for He must be the central figure of every effort; He must abide as the living source of all our virtue.

101

Yet there is an unconscious tendency to avoid the teachings of Christ in favor of some other emphasis from the Scriptures. We make our favorite teaching the cornerstone of our church rather than Jesus. Inevitably we find ourselves attempting to make disciples in our image instead of His.

Jesus said, "The stone which the builders rejected, this became the chief corner stone" (Luke 20:17). It is important to understand that we cannot separate what Jesus says from who Jesus is. Christ and His Word are one. To the degree that we fail to teach what Jesus taught, we are actually rejecting Him as Lord and redefining the dimensions of the cornerstone of the church.

Listen to how the Lord associates Himself with His teachings. He said, "He who rejects Me, and does not receive My sayings, has one who judges him; the word I spoke is what will judge him at the last day" (John 12:48). He warned, "Whoever is ashamed of Me and My words, of him will the Son of Man be ashamed when He comes in His glory" (Luke 9:26). He exposes our hypocrisy, saying, "Why do you call Me 'Lord, Lord,' and do not do what I say?" (Luke 6:46). Christ and His Word are inseparable. Jesus was not a man who became the Word but is the eternal Word who became a man. His very nature is the Word of God. And to reject or ignore what He says is to reject or ignore who He is.

We cannot build the house of the Lord if we do not honor and build upon the full spectrum of Christ's teachings. Unless we are teaching our converts "all that [He] commanded," we are not making disciples (Matt. 28:18); we in our church society will always be trapped in spiritual infancy and religion.

Therefore let us honestly ask ourselves: In the building plan of our churches, how much of an emphasis are we placing upon the words of Jesus? Is there a process in which new converts can become disciples of Christ?

If yours is like most congregations, there is probably little focus given to systematic study and application of Christ's teaching. You see, if Jesus is truly the designer and builder of this house, then we must come to Him for the architectural plans. The building code of the kingdom must be obedience to the words of Christ. "Therefore everyone who hears these words of Mine, and acts upon them, may be compared to a wise man, who built his house upon the rock; and the rain descended, and the floods came, and the winds blew, and burst against that house; and yet it did not fall, for it had been founded upon the rock" (Matt. 7:24-25).

Beloved, there is a storm coming; even now the sky has darkened and the first drops are falling. If we will endure, we must be built upon the rock. Please hear me: you cannot build your house in a storm. It is through the Spirit and words of Christ that the house of the Lord is built. This is exactly what Jesus meant when He said, "I will build My church, and the gates of hell will not prevail against it" (Matt. 16:14).

The Apostolic Foundation

Multitudes of Christians today know what Jesus did yet remain stunted in their spiritual growth. Why? Without realizing it we made the teachings of Paul the cornerstone of the church. The apostle's emphasis centered upon salvation, which faithfully brought us to Jesus. With great wisdom Paul presented God's plan of redemption in Christ. Paul's message revealed what Christ did; but Paul himself was built upon what Christ said. Paul did not become apostle Paul apart from the words of Christ dwelling in him richly.

Yet Jesus alone said He was the way, the truth and the life. Only His words and Spirit are capable of restructuring our souls so that, through conformity to His nature, the Father Himself can make His abode in us (John 14:23). It is this refashioning of our inner man that, upon maturity, establishes us corporately as the house of the Lord.

We are not implying that the rest of the Bible is less anointed or pertinent. It is simply that if the cornerstone is not in place the whole building tends to tilt toward the way we happen to lean.

What we are saying about the priority of Christ's words is in full conformity to the apostolic tradition of the New Testament. Paul writes in 1 Timothy 6:3-6, "If anyone advocates a different doctrine, and does not agree with sound words, those of our Lord Jesus Christ, and with the doctrine conforming to godliness, he is conceited and understands nothing" (vv. 3-4a).

When we seek to build upon a foundation other than Jesus, the results are everything but Jesus. Only Christ can create Christians. If we focus on our "doctrinal novelties," seeking to be just different enough to attract more people than the church down the street, we have missed the entire purpose of both the gospel and the ministry of Christ.

Paul based his teaching "on sound words, those of our Lord Jesus Christ." Look at what John taught: "Watch yourselves, that you might not lose what we have accomplished, but that you may receive a full reward. Anyone who goes too far and does not abide in the teaching of Christ, does not have God" (2 John 8-9a). The priority of this hour is for the church to abide in the teachings and Spirit of the Lord Jesus. From this foundation the house of the Lord will be built.

We have had our pet doctrines and our own particular emphasis. We have been like Peter speaking to Jesus on the Mount of Trans-figuration, "Lord, it is good for us to be here; if You wish, I will make three tabernacles" (Matt. 17:4). We are so ready to offer a plan to God instead of simply hearing and obeying Jesus. I believe the Father Himself has had enough of our ideas and advice. In His love He is interrupting our programs with the same word with which He interrupted Peter: "This is My beloved Son, with whom I am well-pleased; listen to Him!"

Dear Lord, forgive me for following winds of doctrine instead of picking up my cross and following You. Help me now to return with my whole heart to Your words. Lord, I desire to abide in You. I recommit my life to You, and I pray that You alone would be the focal point of all Your people. In Jesus' name, amen.

FIFTEEN

By Wisdom the House Is Built

*T*here was a small city with few men in it and a great king came to it, surrounded it, and constructed large siegeworks against it. But there was found in it a poor wise man and he delivered the city by his wisdom" (Eccl. 9:14-15).

The Fear of the Lord

The wisdom of God can take even a poor man, train him in the ways of the Lord and give him a strategy to deliver a city. Throughout the ages the Lord has had His judges, generals and kings who delivered the nation of Israel. In more modern times God has had His Wesleys, His Martin Luthers, His Jonathan Edwardses, men who turned their countries toward heaven. The chaos of our cities is not greater than the chaos which covered the deep, formless, pre-creation void. God's wisdom brought creation to order, and His wisdom can bring the church back to order as well.

The Lord desires for you to possess His wisdom. How do you find it? "The fear of the Lord is the beginning of wisdom, and the knowledge of the Holy One is understanding" (Prov. 9:10). What is "the fear of the Lord"? It is the human soul, having experienced the crucifixion of self and pride, now trembling in stark vulnerability before almighty God. It is this living awareness: God sees everything. This penetrating discovery marks the holy beginning of finding true wisdom.

However, this perception of the living God is not a terrible reality, for it liberates the mind from the cocoon of carnality, enabling the soul to escape into the Spirit. For all the dynamic gifts through which Jesus revealed the Father's power, His delight was in the fear of the Lord (see Is. 11:1-3). Yes, it is the awe-inspiring wonder of man living in fellowship, not with his religion, but with his God. In such a state the obedient man is invincible.

Indeed, has this not been our problem: The enemy does not fear the church because the church does not fear the Lord? As the fear of the Lord returns to us, the terror of the Lord will be upon our enemies. The fear of the Lord is our wisdom.

Let Wisdom Guide Your Building

"By wisdom a house is built, and by understanding it is established; and by knowledge the rooms are filled with all precious and pleasant riches" (Prov. 24:3-4). The Lord's house is built by wisdom. It is established as we compassionately seek to understand the needs of our brethren. After it is built and established, then knowledge fills the rooms with riches.

You may be asking, Where do I begin? James tells us that if we lack wisdom, we can "ask of God" (James 1:5). Proverbs 4:7 tells us, "The beginning of wisdom is: Acquire wisdom." Wisdom is within the grasp of every man. Ask for wisdom but seek the Lord, for with Him there is sound wisdom stored up for the upright.

Do not panic if wisdom seems far from you. Jesus Himself "kept increasing in wisdom" (Luke 2:52). Ultimately those who knew Him marveled, wondering, "What is this wisdom given to Him?" (Mark 6:2). Jesus grew in wisdom, and so also shall you.

God's Manifold Wisdom

It is the everlasting purpose of God that through the church His "manifold wisdom" might be known "unto the principalities and powers in heavenly places" (Eph. 3:10, KJV). Yes, the Lord has instructed us concerning love. Truly He has apportioned to us an effectual measure of faith. Now He desires to give to His church wisdom.

However, the above scripture speaks of the "manifold" wisdom of God. There are "many folds" to the wisdom of God. Moreover, there is a difference between knowledge and wisdom. We certainly will perish for a lack of knowledge (see Hos. 4:6), but knowledge by itself only puffs up (see 1 Cor. 8:1-2). Wisdom knows what to speak and when to speak it. Knowledge, especially doctrinal knowledge, must be administered through wisdom. Presented by itself even knowledge about unity can be divisive.

Oh, how the church desperately needs men and women in whose mind dwells the wisdom of God, a people who are intimately obedient to the ways of God! We have tried zeal, human ingenuity and ambitious programs, but to little avail. We have endured but not overcome as we had envisioned. Now it is time for those who lack wisdom to ask of God and receive liberally from Him the wisdom to build His house.

The Proper Emphasis of Doctrines

There are doctrines without which we cannot be saved, and there are doctrines which are of lesser importance. "Jesus is Lord" is an unalterable doctrine. "Christ died for sinners" is another. "Jesus Himself is returning" is still another tenet that is essential to true Christian life.

But *when* Jesus returns, whether pre-tribulation, mid-tribulation or post-tribulation, is of lesser importance. As Jesus said, "Be on the alert—for you do not know when the master of the house is coming, whether in the evening, at midnight, at cockcrowing, or in the morning" (Mark 13:35). It simply is not wisdom to argue and divide over when He will return, but rather to remain on the alert. Defining our doctrines is important. We need to clarify our belief systems so our perceptions of truth might be divinely structured and overlaid correctly upon the Scriptures. Without such organization we have little hope of attaining the full benefits of our salvation. However, we can have all the right doctrines and still live outside the presence of God if our hearts are not right. Jesus said, "By this all men will know that you are My disciples, if you have love for one another" (John 13:35).

The outcome of right doctrines is love—love that covers other Christians and builds up the body of Christ; it forgives when offended and serves without hidden motives. It goes extra miles ungrudgingly. If our doctrines are not producing this kind of love, they are a smoke screen that will keep us separate and outside the house of the Lord. Let me give an example. In the first-century church there was a controversy concerning eating meat sacrificed to idols. Paul had his views, while others had theirs (see 1 Cor. 8:8; Acts 15:29; Rev. 2:20). But when he wrote on this subject, he said, "Now concerning things sacrificed to idols, we know that we all have knowledge. Knowledge makes arrogant, but love edifies" (1 Cor. 8:1).

Paul put love *above* knowledge. Everyone had a doctrine or conviction on the subject. In another epistle Paul prayed that the Ephesians would "know the love of Christ, which surpasses all knowledge" (Eph. 3:19). The love of Christ "surpasses all knowledge." Even as Jesus bears with our ignorance because of love, so we must set our priorities according to His love and overlook that which will be more easily communicated as our relationships mature.

It is true that without knowledge we will perish, but knowledge without love is itself a state of perishing. To build the right foundation of the city-church, therefore, we must all be in agreement about Jesus and His command to love one another. Greater wisdom than this will not be given concerning building the house of the Lord.

The Wisdom From Above

There are realistic steps toward seeing prayer and the house of the Lord established in your area. If wisdom shall build the house, it is important to define this dimension of Christ's nature. James 3:17 tells us the wisdom from above "is first pure." We cannot build the Lord's house with selfish or ambitious motives. Our desire should be to see the Lord satisfied. Therefore, our labors must be for Jesus, not self. It must be the love of Christ which compels us, not a desire to rise in prominence among men. Divine wisdom is next "peaceable" (James 3:17). Peacemakers are sons of God; they are men and women of wisdom. Their wisdom lies in their understanding of the sublime and powerful ways of God. This wisdom is not born merely of intellectual study. Rather, because they have accepted the Lord's reproof, truth dwells in their innermost beings. The same eternal voice which brought correction "in the hidden part" is now rewarding them, granting them to "know wisdom" (Ps. 51:6).

The wisdom from above is also gentle and reasonable. We must be more willing to serve than to lead, more willing to be corrected than to teach. Where we see a need such as in the areas of initiating prayer or administration, we should be given to fill the gap. But we must also be quick to surrender our task to any whom the Lord raises without feeling as though we have failed because another more qualified has arrived.

True wisdom is not stubborn but is willing to yield to other ministries and perspectives. It must be unyielding in regard to the deity and centrality of Christ and yet fully aware that God desires all men to be saved; "with gentleness correcting those who are in opposition, if perhaps God may grant them repentance" (2 Tim. 2:24-25).

While the wisdom of God is meek, it is also "unwavering, without hypocrisy." This is wisdom born out of vision, not organizational skills. It is unwavering because it sees that the builder of the house is Christ. It is genuine, "full of mercy and good fruits," overlooking mistakes, helping the weaker churches, disarming suspicion and fear with the credibility of Christ's unfailing love.

Dear Lord, You promised that if we lacked wisdom, You would give it to us liberally. We fear being trapped in our own ways with our own ideas. God grant us wisdom, plans and strategies. Grant us the holy fear of Yourself, that You would become to us wisdom, knowledge and strength. In Jesus' name, amen.

SIXTEEN

The Dynamics of Revival

*I*n a move of God some will be willing to die for what God is doing, and some will be eager to kill them. Nevertheless a great harvest is coming, and it will emerge on a worldwide scale. When it comes, its underlying strength will be a passion for men's souls and the proclamation of a living word from God.

The Lord's Warning

In every generation God has a harvest He seeks to reap through revival. Without fail, however, there will be those who stand in direct opposition to His purpose. In spite of persecution the Lord sends His servants, fully knowing that "some of them they will kill and some they will persecute" (Luke 11:49). We will either receive the word God is speaking or we will seek to kill it.

You may ask, With so much falsehood, how do we know a true stirring of God's Spirit? The answer is not as complex as it seems. Is the message a call to return to Jesus? Is it scriptural and being spoken by more than one voice? Is there a living witness in your own heart that what is spoken is true? Ultimately the ability to discern whether a teaching is truly from God rests in our willingness to obey Him. Regarding His own teaching, Jesus said, "If any man is willing to do His will, he shall know the teaching, whether it is of God, or whether I speak from Myself" (John 7:17).

Assuming a message is genuinely from the Lord, there yet remain many risks. We will have to humble ourselves. There will be opportunities to stumble over the weaknesses of the Lord's servants, or, conversely, we will be tempted to exalt them. There will be suffering, and our motives will be tested. Through it all we will truly discover what is more important to us, the approval of men or of God.

It is an awesome but fearful thing to be a church leader during a time when God is seeking a harvest. In truth, it is not only the harvest which is being weighed but the very soul and character of those in leadership. For in a move of God the gray routine of life ends. Both good and evil gravitate toward a state of fullness, stimulating prophets and "pharisees" alike to their true natures.

Beware of Becoming an "Expert"

Prior to the time of Christ's birth the Pharisees were among the most noble men in the nation. They should have rejoiced in Christ's ministry, but they were instrumental in His death. By the time Jesus' ministry began they were motivated not by their love of God, but by their love of recognition and other personal ambitions. The Pharisees were not the only threat to the moving of God among the people; there were also the "lawyers." While our lawyers are experts in civil law, the lawyers of Jesus' day were experts in Mosaic Law. They explained the Scriptures by drawing support from their own inter-pretations. Because their livelihood was based upon the popularity of their explanations, it was very difficult for them to recant their errors. Instead of repenting, they compounded their doctrinal mistakes by defending them. Thus, they entered deeper into deception.

Like the Pharisees, the men of law found their position in Jewish society being threatened. When anyone is deceived and threatened, he has the potential of becoming dangerous even to the point of demonic possession. He will actually seek to stop a move of God because it endangers him.

Jesus said, "Woe to you lawyers! For you have taken away the key of knowledge; you did not enter in yourselves, and those who were entering in you hindered" (Luke 11:52). The "key" to unlocking the power of knowledge is obedience. If we know spiritual things, we are blessed if we do them (John 13:17). But if we ourselves are not "entering in," we find fault with those God is using. Thus, we cause to stumble those who would have otherwise entered. We become the modern "lawyers" who have "taken away the key of knowledge."

Dynamics of Revival

However, the major hindrance to revival is not the "pharisees" and "lawyers." The main barrier is our own lack of love. It is to our shame that the devil desires men's souls more than does the church. Therefore we must realize that revival will not sweep our land until we possess Christ's passion for the lost. Even in the call to do confrontational spiritual warfare, our authority must spring from a love of souls lest it become simply another wind of doctrine, again blowing us off course.

There are a number of essentials for revival. Here we will consider three of them: compassion, prayer and the proclamation of an anointed word from God. Let us consider the first, Christ's compassion for the lost. God loves the world. We must look at our world in its sinfulness through the same mercy with which Christ gazes upon us. It requires no great insight to perceive the wickedness in our world. Clear vision rests in the heart of the pure: They see God, and, knowing His redemptive mercy, they reach out to the lost.

Indeed, one of our primary objectives in connecting churches is that through our unity Jesus will be revealed. It is Christ's glorious presence in the church, in contrast to the increasing darkness in our cities, which will draw multitudes to Him. Therefore, in all our labors to build the church, we have in our view the "nations" which shall stream to the house of the Lord (see Is. 2:2).

The second essential to revival is prayer. You will remember that the early disciples had been in prayer prior to the outpouring of the Spirit. Afterward they continued in prayer, which released the church into ongoing breakthroughs in God. The will of God is escorted to the earth through prayer. It is as simple as this: Revival is an answer to prayer; if we do not pray, there will be no revival.

The third dynamic which actually lifts revival into a national or worldwide awakening is the proclamation of a living word from God. It is a message anointed with more than just insight or edification. It is truth declared in power. The apostles' message came with such light that upon those who spoke it could truly be stated, "The glory of the Lord [had] risen upon" them. And their words contained such fire that "nations come to [their] light" (Is. 60:1-3).

In the major movings of the Holy Spirit, this anointed proclamation of God's word has typically been a part of the substructure of revival. When John the Baptist stirred the nation of Israel, historians tell us that between 750,000 and 1,000,000 people were baptized through his ministry. What was the origin of such an anointing? "The word of God came to John" (Luke 3:2). It was no mere "teaching" or "fresh insight" which motivated John, but a commission from God to speak His word (John 1:6).

The nature of John's ministry was simple: He was "the voice of one crying in the wilderness" (v. 4). The one crying in the wilderness was the Spirit of God; John was His voice. In preparation for Christ's coming, God Himself was changing the landscape of men's hearts—mountains were coming down, valleys were lifted up. God was doing something, saying something, and John carried the burden of God to the people.

On the day of Pentecost three thousand souls were swept into the kingdom of God. On a natural level there was no mass evangelistic program. The fire of conviction fell under Peter's anointed word.

His message was exactly what God was saying to the world: Jesus rose from the dead; He is the Christ! Thousands were pierced to the heart and immediately changed. God was launching the church; Peter was God's voice.

The Lord has always used His word to shepherd His people out of apostasy, progressively restoring them to the fundamentals of the faith. We should note that, since the Middle or Dark Ages, global awakenings have also brought the church closer to the purity of New Testament order. Consequently, Martin Luther's proclamation that "the just shall live by faith" did more than win the nation of Germany; it restored truth to the church. Wesley's message of his "salvation experience with the witness of the Holy Spirit" not only saved England from a revolution such as the French were experiencing, it brought the church closer to the purity of the gospel.

The majority of the reformers not only kindled revival but were used by God to restore *specific truths* to the body of Christ. As John the Baptist was the voice of one crying in the wilderness, so these men were the voice of God bringing truth back to the church. The glory of the Lord had risen upon them, and nations came to their light (see Is. 60:1-3).

The message that brings worldwide awakening is that which embodies what God is doing and proclaims what God is saying. The revivalists not only brought souls to Christ but also the next phase in God's progressive renewal and restoration of the church. None of those who impacted nations presented new or extra-biblical revelation; they brought anointed, *scriptural* truth to their generations.

Even today God's truth continues "marching on." What is the Lord doing today? It is obvious that over the past years the Holy Spirit has been dissolving denominational walls between churches. The writings of contemporary Christian authors from many perspectives have been homogenized into our spiritual diet. In general, Christians today are less and less the product of one denomination. Additionally, different church affiliations have found themselves standing side-by-side fighting common enemies such as abortion, pornography and the occult.

Where is all this going? A wonderful dawn is breaking upon the church. While we have grown under the same teachers and fought against the same enemies, to our amazement we are discovering, in different ways, that the Lord has been guiding us all to Himself. This, we believe, is the anointed truth which God is speaking: It is time for the house of the Lord to be built. As Jesus steps forth from His house, revival will break forth in many cities.

Our Strategy From God

While the harvest field of this coming revival is worldwide, we recognize that the specific battlegrounds are cities. In the book of Revelation Jesus dealt individually with churches in certain cities. Each church had a unique struggle as well as unique promises. You will also remember that the Israelites conquered the promised land city by city. Therefore, for us to touch a nation, we must focus upon its cities.

We are called to serve as a witness to confirm and help establish the praying, Christ-centered church. We have seen that a divided church cannot win the war for its city. And we know that corporate prayer is always the prerequisite for revival. Therefore, a citywide visitation of Christ is impossible until at least some measure of that city's churches are committed to pray for revival.

Although many churches will continue to be blessed of God independently of the citywide anointing, to impact the heavenly places and win the war for our regions we must be united in prayer. The spiritual void in the heavenlies, which gave room to the powers of darkness in the first place, must be filled by the maturing, united body of Christ. God's focus is uniquely upon this ripening, praying church. Without any doubt, from the house of the Lord revival will burst upon our land.

Heavenly Father, grant us Your vision for revival! Open our eyes to Your strategies and wisdom, Your love and compassion. Help us not to be caught fighting what You are doing. We give ourselves to serving You in the simplicity of devotion to Christ. We commit ourselves to build Your house. In Jesus' name, amen.

SEVENTEEN

Spiritual Authority and the Things We Love

*W*hile the doctrines of Christianity can be taught, Christlike-ness can only be inspired. This next generation of leaders will by their humble and holy lives inspire multitudes. They will truly walk in Christ's love; they will be granted great authority.

Authority to Make Disciples

There are many administrators but few examples of Christ; many teachers but few who walk as Jesus walked. Indeed, while many stand in leadership today, not many function in Christ's authority.

However, a new level of authority is coming to the church. The Holy Spirit is about to crown God's servants with anointed spiritual authority; it will bring healing and deliverance on a scale unprecedented since the first century. In fact, God's promise is that in some cases entire cities will taste salvation.

Spiritual authority is nothing less than God Himself confirming our words with His power. The examples in the Scriptures are plain: Those who are raised up by God are backed up by God. They will "decree a thing and it will be established" (Job 22:28). As He did for Samuel, the Lord will let none of their words fall to the ground, for their words and their authority will be a manifestation of the living God Himself.

Yet why is there so little true spiritual authority in the church today? The answer lies partly in the fact that the authority of the church has been delegated to it, given only to carry out the purposes of God, and not to accomplish man-made programs and traditions. What are God's purposes? Jesus said, "All authority has been given to Me in heaven and on earth. Go therefore and make disciples of all the nations" (Matt. 28:18-19).

Christ gave the church authority to make disciples, not merely converts. Many are believers in Jesus, but few are followers of Him. How do we make disciples? Jesus answers that for us: "teaching them to observe all that I commanded" (Matt. 28:19-20). When the church returns to teaching all that Jesus taught, our disciples will have authority to do all that Jesus did.

This new level of authority is not something we possess merely because we strive for it. We cannot buy it as Simon the magician attempted to do (see Acts 8:18). The power of authority will not function simply because we copy the methods of another, as the sons of Sceva realized (see Acts 19:14); nor can it be attained automatically because we read books about building the church. We cannot pretend to have spiritual authority. There are, however, divinely ordained ways for us to minister in Christ's authority.

Authority to Lay Down Our Lives

From the beginning of our salvation we have enjoyed the Father's unconditional love. As we mature, however, there comes a time when the Father's love toward us seems conditional. As it was for Christ, so it is for those who follow Him. He said, "For this reason the Father loves Me, because I lay down My life" (John 10:17). Jesus lived in the deepest intimacies of the Father's love because He laid down His life for the sheep. If we will grow in true authority, we will do so by laying down our lives for His sheep.

Have you felt the drawing, the divine working of the Father bringing you into Christlike surrender? Be encouraged; He is equipping you for this next outpouring of His Spirit. But also be advised: Your authority will be an outgrowth of your life laid down in love.

Perhaps we have been misled in our understanding of what spiritual authority is and where it comes from. We do not move in true spiritual authority simply because we hold a position in the church. Here is the path to true spiritual authority: The Holy Spirit delivers us from our fears and restores to us the possession of our souls. Then, without being intimidated by the enemy or manipulated by the influence of man, we choose to lay down our lives in obedience to God. Yes, in full freedom, with avenues of escape plainly within our grasp, we fearlessly surrender our souls to the Almighty. No one controls us but God, yet our lives are laid down, like Christ's, for the sins of men.

When we could easily fight and win, yet turn the other cheek; when we are unjustly opposed, yet quietly endure—at those moments spiritual authority is entering our lives.

"No man has taken [My life] away from Me, but I lay it down on My own initiative" (John 10:18). Jesus was not forced to accept crucifixion; He *chose* crucifixion. Christ's Gethsemane prayer was not an entreaty to escape the cross, for while Jesus was still in the garden He told Peter, "Do you think that I cannot appeal to My Father and He will at once put at My disposal more than twelve legions of angels?" (Matt. 26:53). Jesus had a choice: legions of warring angels and immediate personal deliverance, or death on the cross and deliverance for the world. He chose to die. The willful decision to lay down our lives as Jesus did is the very path upon which true authority develops. Jesus said, "I have authority to lay [My life] down" (John 10:18). His authority came in the laying down

119

of His life. Our authority comes from the same source: picking up our cross and laying down our lives.

Authority, Not Control

Spiritual authority is the power and provision of God to invade and transform the temporal with the power of the eternal. It is not something our flesh can imitate, nor is it found in the tone of our words or the gaze of our eyes. Divine authority requires divine sanction. This sanction comes from passing the tests of love.

When authority is administered without love, it degenerates into control. God does not call us to control His people but to inspire and guard them. The outcome of control is oppression, witchcraft and strife. But the result of love is liberty and the power to build up and protect God's people.

In spiritual authority there is no control involved, nor is any needed. Our lives and the lives of those who follow us are laid down, like Christ's, on our own initiative. It is a choice born out of love. Since true authority itself is born in freedom, freedom is what it breeds.

We will walk in either the true authority of love, the false authority of control or no authority at all. Both false authority and no authority are rooted in fear, and we react to fear in either of two ways. The first reaction, which produces false authority, is to seek to control those around us, thus making the circumstances around us more predictable and less threatening. The other response to fear is to refuse to accept and exercise any authority at all. Many relationships are simply the pairing of these symbionic needs: the desire to control and the willingness to be controlled. Both are fueled by overreactions to fear.

The Scripture tells us, however, "There is no fear in love; but perfect love casts out fear" (1 John 4:18). Since true authority is built upon love, its goal is to liberate, not dominate. Therefore, before one can truly move in spiritual authority he must be delivered from fear and its desire to control; he must be rooted and grounded in love.

Authority to Inspire Christlikeness

When our teaching about God and our obedience to Him are one, spiritual authority accompanies our lives. Jesus astounded the multitudes, for He spoke "as one having authority" (Matt. 7:28-29). What He taught was consistent with how He lived. Therefore, we also must live and display the virtue we seek to teach.

If we seek to train our church to pray, we ourselves must first be intercessors. You may say, But out of a congregation of several hundred, only three people join me for prayer. Then those three are the individuals you are truly touching. Do not be discouraged, for you will win others. But the measure of our success is not the numbers in attendance Sunday mornings. God has given us people so we may train them, not merely count them. Of this group those whom we inspire to live like Christ are actually the measure of our success, the test of our effectiveness in the ministry.

You may say, But I've never been a leader. When anyone lays down his or her life in Christ's love, others will see and follow. Such a one can speak with confidence and penetration whether he is a pastor, a housewife or a child. This next generation will not just teach the people; they will inspire the body of Christ to live like Jesus. Their example in all things will awaken godliness in those around them. From true virtue shall the leaders of tomorrow draw true authority, for when the nature of Christ is revealed, the authority of Christ soon follows.

Authority Born From Love

As wide as our sphere of love is, to that extent we have spiritual authority. We see this in the mother who loves her child. Such a woman has authority to protect, train and nurture her offspring. She has authority to protect what she loves. The same is true of the husband over his family. His authority is not merely to rule but to establish his home in the life of Christ. True spiritual authority is born of love.

The individuals who love their local church have authority to build up that church. Their authority is not extended, however, beyond the boundaries of their love. If we love the entire body of Christ in a locale, our authority touches the lives of those in our city or region, either through the burden of prayer or through teaching or service.

The testing ground of all spiritual things is love, for love alone purifies our motives and delivers us from the deceitfulness of self. Even authority in warfare must be rooted in love. David gained the skills to slay Goliath by defending his father's sheep from vicious predators; he did not learn these skills on the battlefield. He loved the sheep so much that he would even risk his life for them. So also we grow in authority as we protect our Father's sheep, the flock He has given us to love.

Authority is muscle in the arm of love. The more one loves, the more authority is granted to him. If we love our cities and are willing to lay down our lives for them, God will enlarge our hearts, granting us authority to confront principalities and powers.

However, no man should ever engage in confrontational warfare who does not love what he has been called to protect. If you do not love your city, do not pray against the ruling forces of darkness. Satan knows the genuineness of our love by the brightness of the glory which surrounds us. A man without Christlike love will soon shrink back and fail in spiritual warfare.

Therefore, in His mercy God restrains most Christians from understanding the doctrines of our authority in spiritual warfare. For there are many things He has to say which we are not able to hear until the base of our love is expanded. In His love He protects us from presumptuously attacking the strongholds of hell and suffering loss. Yet if we are truly anointed in God's love, the price to see our cities saved is not too great, for it is the price love always pays: the willingness to die for what we care for.

Authority to Build up the Body of Christ

"For even if I should boast somewhat further about our authority, which the Lord gave for building you up and not for destroying you" (2 Cor. 10:8).

Many so-called "prophets" today think they are called, like Jeremiah, to "pluck up and to break down, to destroy and to overthrow" (Jer. 1:10). Jeremiah's message was to a people who were destined to be carried off into Babylon. He spoke to a people who did not have the Holy Spirit and the blood of Jesus, a nation whom God Himself said was destined for captivity (see Jer. 12:7).

The whole commission of Jeremiah, though, was more than confronting sin. It also included promises of restoration and deliverance, "to build and to plant" (Jer. 1:10). To represent the heart of the Lord, which is the true prophetic role, the servant of God must know if the Holy Spirit is preparing to destroy or seeking to rebuild.

Today we are a people coming out of captivity, a people whom God is encouraging to build, as they did in the days of Nehemiah, Ezra, Haggai and Zechariah. We have been in exile from the promises of God, but we are returning to rebuild the Lord's house. It is not a time to tear down the body of Christ; it is time to establish and to build up.

The authority coming to the church in this next outpouring will be to restore the local, citywide church. Like Paul's authority, ours will be given for building and encouraging and not for destroying.

God has this new leadership constantly before His eyes. Pastors from many denominations, along with their congregations, are meeting together in prayer, seeking to draw the very fire and heart of God into their souls. Emerging from this foundation of humility and prayer is a new authority to make disciples of Christ. Because their love encompasses the entire city, their authority reaches even into the heavenly places. They are beginning to impact the spiritual atmosphere of their cities; in many cases they are becoming effective against the principalities and powers ruling there. These are the leaders God is raising up, whom He will back up with His power.

Dear Lord, make me a willing sacrifice. I desire Your authority, Lord. Give me courage to surrender in obedience, even when I do not see the outcome and when all I see is loss. Help me to trust as I walk through the narrow gate. Establish in me Your love that I might defend Your people with authority. In Jesus' name, amen.

EIGHTEEN

The House
of Glory

L ord, we consecrate ourselves as priests unto You; we sanctify ourselves without regard to divisions. Build us together with those who love You. Make us a living temple, and then draw all men, even all nations, unto Yourself.

When Glory Filled the Temple

The dedication of Solomon's temple offers us a picture of what God is seeking in the church. The temple was built, and in great pageantry and celebration it was consecrated to the Lord. Solomon offered a sacrifice of 22,000 oxen and 120,000 sheep. Then, immediately after the king prayed, the glory of God was manifested in full view of the people for the first time in over four hundred years. We read, "Fire came down from heaven and consumed the burnt offering and the sacrifices; and the glory of the Lord filled the house" (2 Chron. 7:1).

The Lord honored the dedication of the stone temple with a visible unveiling of His glory. How much more does He seek to reveal His glorious presence in His living temple, the church? Be assured, before the skies part and the Lord Jesus Himself returns, the outraying of His divine presence shall rise upon us, and His glory shall be seen upon us (see Is. 60:1-3).

Do you doubt such an unfolding of God's will? I tell you, according to the very pattern of the Lord in the Scriptures, a dispensational moving of God has *always* revealed His glory. Abraham saw His glory; Moses dwelt in His glory; Job, David, Isaiah and Ezekiel all beheld His glory. The seventy elders "saw the God of Israel; and under His feet there appeared to be a pavement of sapphire, as clear as the sky itself. Yet He did not stretch out His hand against the nobles of the sons of Israel; and they beheld God, and they ate and drank" (Ex. 24:10). Not just the prophets of Israel, but all seventy nobles as well beheld God—they ate and drank of His glory. Indeed, the entire nation followed the cloud of glory by day and observed the pillar of His fire by night; they saw His awesome splendor (see Ex. 24:17; Lev. 9:23; Num. 14:10).

In a dispensational moving of God it is inconceivable that the glory of God *not* be revealed. In this overlap of two distinct epochs, in this conflict of the ages, the God of glory shall be manifested both in the nations and in His people. Indeed, He is coming to be glorified in His saints and marveled at by those who believe (see 2 Thess. 1:10).

But the way into that glory, the preparation for it, is occurring now in our obedience to the Lord and in our becoming His house. You see, there were prerequisites which occurred prior to the Lord's appearance in Solomon's temple.

First, it was not until the temple was actually built, with all its separate aspects connected and covered in gold, that the glory of the Lord appeared. Likewise, we also must be built together and "perfected in unity" if we would see the fullness of the Lord displayed among us. As Peter tells us, we must corporately become "living stones...built up as a spiritual house...a holy priesthood" before Christ will honor us with His glory (1 Pet. 2:5).

The next requirement concerns our worship. The Lord was not revealed until the singers, trumpeters and priests lifted their voices in praise and worship to God. We cannot overstate the need to be worshippers of God. Even now in a number of corporate church services a faint, luminous glory is appearing. It is the living cloud of His presence. As He begins to take His place as King among us, He is literally being enthroned upon the praises of His people.

However, there was another dimension of preparation which also preceded the revelation of glory. It pertained to those in leadership. The text reads, "And when the priests came forth from the holy place (for all the priests who were present had sanctified themselves, without regard to divisions)...then the house, the house of the Lord, was filled with a cloud, so that the priests could not stand to minister because of the cloud, for the glory of the Lord filled the house of God" (2 Chron. 5:11-14).

When the priests entered the holy place, they "sanctified themselves without regard to divisions" (v. 11). The priestly divisions had been ordained by God according to individual families and unique purposes. But when it came to building the temple and entering the holy place, the priest had to disregard the lesser place of service to enter the greater place of divine presence.

So also today, "without regard to divisions," churches are entering the holy place of Christ's glory. In cities throughout North America and the world literally thousands of pastors are surrendering their lives in acts of holy consecration. The outcome? The church is being "fitted together...growing into a holy temple in the Lord; in whom [we] also are being built together into a dwelling of God in the Spirit" (Eph. 2:21-22).

Notice these words: "fitted together...built together." The true house of the Lord is only revealed when the church, without regard to divisions, is fitted together. Only then can we truly become the temple of the Lord, "a dwelling of God in the Spirit."

The Source of Glory

Jesus prayed, "And the glory which Thou hast given Me I have given to them; that they may be one, just as We are one; I in them, and Thou in Me, that they may be perfected in unity" (John 17:22-23). Jesus is not coming to give us a new form of church government or new doctrines and programs. As we stated, He is coming to be glorified in His saints (2 Thess. 1:10). It was for this that He called us, that we may gain His glory (2 Thess. 2:14).

Let us each see that God is building something in this hour which will far exceed our current definition of the church. God is building us together into "a holy temple in the Lord," a place where His very glory shall be revealed.

This next prayer is perhaps the most important in this book. It is our response to God's call to build His house. It is uniquely directed toward those who are pastors, church leaders and intercessors, to build "without regard to divisions." If you are a leader, and you see the vision of the house of the Lord, please pray with us.

Dear Lord, I thank You for granting me a new opportunity to serve You. I repent of the areas in my heart where I have allowed division and self-interest to guide my actions. Lord, I want to see Your glory, even to abide as Moses did in Your sacred presence. Master, I consecrate my heart, without regard to divisions, to Your sacred service. Before You I sanctify my life and my church to build the house of the Lord in my city. In Jesus' name, amen.

PART FOUR

Our Strategy:
Obedience to Christ

When Israel was united in its obedience to the Lord,
it did not matter how many or how strong their enemies were;
they were invincible in war. God fought for them. When the
church is obedient to Christ, God will fight for us as well.

*"Hear, O Israel, you are approaching the battle
against your enemies today. Do not be fainthearted.
Do not be afraid, or panic, or tremble before them,
for the Lord your God is the one who goes with you,
to fight for you against your enemies, to save you."*
Deuteronomy 20:3-4

NINETEEN

Exposing the Accuser of the Brethren

*M*ore churches have been destroyed by the accuser of the brethren and its faultfinding than by either immorality or misuse of church funds. So prevalent is this influence in our society that, among many, faultfinding has been elevated to the status of a "ministry." The Lord has promised, however, that in His house accusing one another will be replaced with prayer, and faultfinding will be replaced with a love that covers a multitude of sins.

Satan Wants to Stop Your Growth

This chapter is written specifically to expose the activity of the accuser of the brethren among born-again Christians. There are individuals who are trapped in cults where mind-control and deception are involved; we are not dealing with the uniqueness of their problems in this study. Rather our goal is to see the living church delivered from the stronghold of faultfinding and to have our hearts turned instead to prayer.

In an attempt to hinder if not altogether halt the next move of God, Satan has sent forth an army of faultfinding demons against the church. The purpose of this assault is to entice the body of Christ away from the perfections of Jesus and onto the imperfections of one another.

The faultfinder spirit's assignment is to assault relationships on all levels. It attacks families, churches and interchurch associations, seeking to bring irreparable schisms into our unity. Masquerading as discernment, this spirit will slip into our opinions of other people, leaving us critical and judgmental. Consequently, we all need to evaluate our attitude toward others. If our thoughts are other than "faith working through love," we need to be aware that we may be under spiritual attack.

The faultfinder demon will incite individuals to spend days and even weeks unearthing old faults or sins in their minister or church. The people who are held captive by this deceitful spirit become "crusaders," irreconcilable enemies of their former assemblies. In most cases the things they deem wrong or lacking are the very areas in which the Lord seeks to position them for intercession. What might otherwise be an opportunity for spiritual growth and meeting a need becomes an occasion of stumbling and withdrawal. In truth, their criticisms are a smoke screen for a prayerless heart and an unwillingness to serve.

That someone should discover the imperfections of their pastor or church is by no means a sign of spirituality. Indeed, we were able to find fault with the church *before* we were Christians! What we do with what we see, however, is the measure of Christlike maturity. Remember, when Jesus saw the condition of mankind, He "emptied Himself, taking the form of a bondservant....He humbled Himself by becoming obedient to death, even death on a cross" (Phil. 2:7-8)). He died to take away sins; He did not just judge them.

No One Is Exempt

It is of some consolation that Christ Himself could not satisfy the "standards" of this spirit when it spoke through the Pharisees. No matter what Jesus did, the Pharisees found fault with Him.

If you personally have not consulted with and listened to the individual of whom you are critical, how can you be sure that you are not fulfilling the role of the accuser of the brethren? Even the "Law does not judge a man, unless it first hears from him" (John 7:51).

The enemy's purpose in this assault is to discredit the minister so it can discredit his message. I have personally listened to scores of pastors from many denominational backgrounds, and I have found that the timing of this spirit's attack upon their congregations was almost always just prior to or immediately after a significant breakthrough. The unchallenged assault of this demon *always* stopped the forward progress of their church.

When this spirit infiltrates an individual's mind, its accusations come with such venom and intimidation that even those who should know better are bewildered and then seduced by its influence. Nearly all involved take their eyes off Jesus and focus upon "issues," ignoring during the contention that Jesus is actually praying for His body to become one. Beguiled by this demon, accusations and counter accusations rifle through the soul of the congregation, stimulating suspicion and fear among the people. Devastation wracks the targeted church, while discouragement blankets and seeks to destroy the pastor and his family or other servants of God in the church.

Nearly every minister reading this has faced the assault of the faultfinder spirit at one time or another. Each has known the depression of trying to track down this accusing spirit as it whispers its gossip through the local church: Trusted friends seem distant, established relationships are shaken, and the vision of the church is quagmired in strife and inaction.

This enemy is not limited to attacks on local churches, however. Its attacks are also citywide and national. Major publishers have made millions of dollars selling defaming books which are hardly more credible than gossip columns in the tabloids. Yes, in a few of the ministries there was serious sin, but there are biblical ways to bring correction, ways which lead to healing and not to destruction. There are denominational supervisors as well as local ministerial associations that can review disputes privately. Instead, church leaders boldly challenge other leaders; newsletters and cassette tapes critical of various ministries circulate like poison through the blood-stream of the body of Christ—and how the Savior's church glut-tonously eats it up!

To mask the diabolical nature of its activity, the faultfinder will often garb its criticisms in religious clothing. Under the pretense of protecting sheep from a "gnat-sized" error in doctrine, it forces the flock to swallow a "camel-sized" error of loveless correction. Attempting to correct violations of Scripture, the very methods employed are a violation of Scripture. Where is the "spirit of gentleness" of which Paul speaks in Galatians 6:1, the humility in "looking to yourselves, lest you too be tempted"? Where is the love motive to "restore such a one"?

In most cases the person supposedly in error has never even been contacted before his alleged mistakes enter the rumor mill of the cities' churches. Only then, after the slander has been made public through a book, tape or media broadcast, does he become aware of his alleged faults. Brethren, the spirit behind such accusations must be discerned, for its motive is not to restore and heal but to destroy.

The Pure Example

The church needs correction, but the ministry of reproof must be patterned after Christ and not the accuser of the brethren. When Jesus corrected the churches in Asia (see Rev. 2-3), He sandwiched His rebuke between praise and promises. He reassured the churches that the voice about to expose their sin was the very voice which inspired their virtue. After encouraging them, He then brought correction.

Even when a church was steeped in error, as was the case with two of the seven churches, Christ still offered grace for change. How patient was Jesus? He even gave "Jezebel...time to repent" (Rev. 2:20-21). After He admonished a church, His last words were not condemnation but promises.

Is this not His way with each of us? Even in the most serious corrections the voice of Jesus is always the embodiment of "grace and truth" (John 1:14). Jesus said of the sheep, "They know his voice. And a stranger they simply will not follow, but will flee from him" (John 10:4,5). Remember, if the word of rebuke or correction does not offer grace for restoration, it is not the voice of your Shepherd. If you are one of Christ's sheep, you will flee from it.

The Enemy's Weapons

To find an indictment against the church, it is important to note the enemy must draw his accusations from hell. If we have repented of our sins, no record of them nor of our mistakes exists in heaven. As it is written, "Who will bring a charge against God's elect? God is the one who justifies" (Rom. 8:33). Jesus is not condemning us but is at the Father's right hand interceding on our behalf.

Let us, therefore, expose the weapons of the faultfinder. The first is our actual sins. Our failure to repent when the Holy Spirit desires to correct us opens the door for the accuser to condemn us. The voice of the enemy never offers hope nor extends grace for repentance. It acts as though it is the voice of God and we are guilty of the "unpardonable sin." The way to defeat the enemy in this arena is to disarm him by sincerely repenting of the sin, looking again to the atonement of Christ as the sum of all our righteousness.

Yet Satan seeks not only to accuse us as individuals but to blend into our minds criticisms and condemnation against others as well. Instead of praying for one another, we react in the flesh against offenses. Our un-Christlike responses are then easily manipulated by the faultfinder spirit.

Therefore, we cast down the accuser of the brethren by learning to pray *for* one another instead of preying *on* one another. We must learn to forgive in the same manner as Christ has forgiven us. If one

135

has repented of his sins, we must exercise the same attitude of "divine forgetfulness" that exists in heaven. We defeat the faultfinder when we emulate the nature of Jesus: as a lamb, Christ died for sinners; as a priest, He intercedes.

The second weapon this demon uses against us is our past mistakes and poor decisions. Each of us has an inherent propensity toward ignorance. One does not have to read far into the history of the saints to discover they were not called because of their intrinsic wisdom. In truth, we all have made mistakes. Hopefully we have at least learned from them and developed humility because of them. This faultfinding demon, however, takes our past mistakes and parades them before our memory, criticizing our efforts to do God's will, thus keeping us in bondage to the past.

When the enemy pits us against one another, it first provokes us to jealousy or fear. The security of our place in life seems threatened by another's success. Perhaps to justify our personal failures or flaws, we magnify the past shortcomings of others. The more our jealousy grows the more this demon exploits our thoughts, until *nothing* about the individual or his church seems right.

In the final stage we actually wage a campaign against him. No defense he offers will satisfy us. We are convinced he is deceived and dangerous; and we think it is up to us to warn others. Yet the truth is the person whose mind is controlled by the faultfinder demon is the one who is deceived and dangerous. For his own unrepentant thoughts toward jealousy and fleshly criticism have supplied hell with a "lumber yard" of material to erect walls between members of the body of Christ.

Sadly, it is often leaders who fall from the intensity of their first love and become the fiercest persecutors of others who are moving in the Holy Spirit. Christ's disciples will be persecuted, but this author can find no biblical authorization for Christians to persecute others. Persecution is a deed of the flesh. "But as at that time he who was born according to the flesh persecuted him who was born according to the Spirit, so it is now also" (Gal. 4:29). Incredibly, those who are given to persecuting others often actually think they are "offering service to God" (John 16:2).

To combat this enemy we must create an atmosphere of grace among us as individuals and between us as churches. Like the Father who has given us life, we must seek to cause all things to work together for good. If one stumbles we must be quick to cover him, without condoning hypocrisy, for we are "members of one another" (Eph. 4:25). As it is written, "None of you shall approach any blood relative of his to uncover nakedness; I am the Lord" (Lev. 18:6). We are family, begotten from one Father. "Their nakedness you shall not uncover; for their nakedness is yours" (v. 10). Even under the old covenant it was unlawful to uncover another's mistake publicly. Love finds a redemptive way to cover a multitude of sins.

Where the Vultures Are Gathered

The accuser uses yet another weapon, and it uses this weapon astutely. There are times in our walk with God when, to increase fruitfulness, the Father prunes us back (see John 15). This is a season of preparation during which the Lord's purpose is to lead His servants into new power in ministry. This growth process requires new levels of surrender as well as a fresh crucifixion of the flesh. It is often a time of humiliation and testing, of emptiness and seeming ineffectiveness as God expands our dependency upon Him. It can be a fearful time when our need is exposed in stark visibility.

Unfortunately, this time of weakness is apparent not only to the man or woman of God; it frequently occurs before the church and before principalities and powers as well. The faultfinder spirit, and those who have come to think as it thinks, find in their target's vulnerability an opportunity to crush him.

Time and again, what would otherwise become an incubator of life becomes a coffin of death. Those who might otherwise emerge with the clarity and power of prophetic vision are beaten down and abandoned, cut off from the very people who should have prayed them through to resurrection. In this attack the faultfinder is most destructive. For here this demon aborts the birth of mature ministries, those who would arm their churches for war.

The faultfinders and gossips are already planted in the church—

perhaps *you* are such a one! When the living God is making your pastor more deeply dependent, and thus more easily shaped for His purposes, do you criticize his apparent lack of anointing? Although he did not abandon you during your time of need, do you abandon him now when your faith might be the very encouragement he needs to yield to the cross?

Those who are sympathetic to the accuser of the brethren fulfill, by application, Matthew 24:28: "Wherever the corpse is, there the vultures will gather." The backbiting of these vulture-like individuals actually feeds their lower nature, for they seek what is dead in a church; they are *attracted* to what is dying.

Eventually these faultfinders depart, instinctively looking to take issue with some other church. "These are grumblers, finding fault...the ones who cause divisions" (Jude 16-19). They leave behind former brethren severely wounded and in strife, and a pastor greatly disheartened. Soon they join a new church, and in time God begins to deal with this new pastor. Once again the faultfinder spirit manifests itself, strategically positioned to destroy another church.

Today God is seeking to raise up His servants with increased power and authority. In the pruning stage of their growth, will we water their dryness with prayer, or will we be vultures drawn to devour their dying flesh?

How to Correct Error

When the accuser comes, it brings distorted facts and condemnation. Those who are trapped by this spirit never research the *virtues* in the organization or person they are attacking. With the same zeal that the faultfinders seek to unearth sin, those who will conquer this enemy must earnestly seek God's heart and His calling for those they would reprove. True correction, therefore, will proceed with *reverence,* not *revenge.* Indeed, are not those whom we seek to correct Christ's servants? Are they not His possession? Is it possible the works of which we are jealous, and thus critical, might be the very works of Christ? Also, let us ask ourselves: Why has God chosen *us* to bring His rebuke? Are we walking in Christ's pattern?

These are important questions, for to be anointed with Christ's authority to rebuke we must be committed to men with Christ's love. But if we are angry, embittered or jealous toward another, we cannot even pray correctly for that person, much less reprove him. Jesus, the great Lion of Judah, was declared worthy to bring forth judgment by virtue of His nature: He was a Lamb slain for men's sin. *If we are not determined to die for men, we have no right to judge them.*

Those who seek to justify leaving a church must not do so simply through finding fault. Rather we should openly communicate with the ministerial team. Our attitude should be one of prayer and love, leaving a blessing for what we gained by our time spent in the church. If there has indeed been sin in the ministry, we should contact the church authorities in the city and leave the situation with them.

Additionally, local ministers should be in communication with one another, never basing their opinion of another church or leader on the testimony of one who has just left it. If people join your congregation and bring with them a root of bitterness against their former assembly, that root will spring up in your church, and many will be defiled. Therefore, no matter how much you need new members, never build your congregation with individuals who are unreconciled to their former fellowship.

Indeed, the Lord's word to us is that in the house of the Lord criticism must be replaced with prayer, and faultfinding eliminated with a covering love. Where there is error, we must go with a motive to restore. Where there are wrong doctrines, let us maintain a gentle spirit, correcting those in opposition.

Dear Lord, forgive us for our lack of prayer and the weakness of our love. Master, we want to be like You, that when we see a need, instead of criticizing, we lay down our lives for it. Lord, heal Your church of this demonic stronghold! In Jesus' name, amen.

TWENTY

God's
Strategy for
Our Cities

*E*ven *as the Father had a plan of redemption which required Christ to go to the cross, He also has a plan for our cities. The strategy of our warfare is not to bind principalities and powers randomly or repetitively as is the habit of some; rather we are to seek God until we have His plan, and then, as an army, we are to follow Jesus.*

God Has a Strategy for Your Area

There is only one plan which will win our cities. God has it, and we must seek Him to receive it. Since Jesus already warned that "a house divided against itself shall not stand" (Matt. 12:25), the first strategy for the believing church is that they be united. Then the outworking of our unity must result in the citywide church becoming the house of prayer. Emerging from Christ-centered unity and Christ-initiated prayer will be God's unique strategy for our cities.

Our confidence is that God does have a plan for our cities. Even as Christ did not operate out of a general benevolence toward men, only doing the things He saw the Father do, so we also must seek God until we are following His plan.

Whether we are aware of it or not, the Father always operates strategically in His affairs with men. Who among us has not stood in awe as the Lord orchestrated people, purposes and events with eternal precision—a bill was paid, a word spoken, a gift given at just the right time? As the Father's wisdom unfolds, we will become aware that God is working continually on many levels at once. The seeming insignificance of our actions or prayers is part of a multi-faceted strategy from God, and they are an aspect in the overall success of His plan. Therefore, whatever He says to do, no matter how small, we should do it, trusting in the greatness of His wisdom.

When Jesus sent the seventy disciples to drive out demons from men, Christ Himself was positioned in a higher realm, "watching Satan fall from heaven like lightning" (Luke 10:18). On one level, the disciples were warring against demons; on another, Jesus was warring against Satan.

Again, when Jesus sent out His seventy disciples, there was a divine wisdom governing their movement. The disciples were not traveling randomly about Israel. Rather they were sent specifically to cities where Jesus would soon visit (see Luke 10:1). It was actually in context of being integrated into the overall strategy of God that Jesus gave His disciples authority "over all the power of the enemy" (Luke 10:19). Their authority was not independent from obedience to Christ, but because of it. It was a small part of a greater whole.

The disciples could not, as a rule, use their authority indiscriminately against the enemy the way Christians attempt to bind a principality today. No. They were united together under Jesus. He issued the commands and gave them authority in context with the commands.

Obedience, Virtue and Power

"You are strong, and the word of God abides in you, and you have overcome the evil one" (1 John 2:14). The Lord is again raising up an army. To become strong like these young men John addressed, we must also abide in Christ's word. The Word of God is a two-edged sword; that is, there are two aspects of the Word, each as sharp as the other. The first is the *established* will of God, which comes through knowing the Scriptures. The second is the *communicated* will of God, which comes through our relationship with the Lord.

Obedience to both dimensions of the Word is essential for successful spiritual warfare. However, before God leads us to take our cities, He will inevitably lead us into the desert. Here, in a wilderness of weaknesses and temptations, obedience to each edge of the sword is tested and refined; here is where the power of God comes forth.

This time of testing may come to us as individuals, singular churches or as a citywide church. Regardless, we must pass God's tests before we graduate into power. Thus, our concept of being "Spirit-filled" must adjust to include this dimension of testing and warfare. For in this hour many who are truly filled with the Holy Spirit will likewise find themselves facing battles that God has allowed to prove their character. The disciple of Christ should note carefully: Our greatest spiritual growth occurs when no one is looking, when we feel even God has withdrawn from us.

We see both the pattern of God's dealings and the wisdom of His ways in Christ. "Then Jesus was led up by the Spirit into the wilderness to be tempted by the devil" (Matt. 4:1). Jesus had just been baptized by John when the heavens opened, and the voice of God audibly affirmed the Father's pleasure in His Son. We would expect that after this a glorious ministry would begin, but instead Jesus was led by the Holy Spirit into a direct encounter with Satan in the wilderness. Here the very word the Father had spoken concerning Christ's sonship was tested by the devil.

Christians need to accept that the Father is not squeamish about testing His sons and daughters. The word "tempted" in this text means "proven or tested through adversity." God led Jesus *to be tested in spiritual warfare with the devil himself!* Mark's account adds that this happened immediately after the baptism of John, and that Jesus was impelled into the desert by the Spirit; Luke's Gospel states that Jesus was "full of the Holy Spirit" during this test. This was not a matter of His flesh falling into temptation, but His character being proven in temptation. Christ was tempted as we are (see Heb. 4:15), in His mind, with weakness washing over His soul. To perfect character, the temptations we experience must be *real* temptations which lead us to *real* choices. The doubts must have legitimate questions; the fleshly temptations must have credible pleasures. Yet in the face of what Satan hurls, we must remain loyal to God.

The outcome of this testing was that "Jesus returned to Galilee in the power of the Spirit" (Luke 4:14). After success in warfare came a level of power which brought healing for every disease and illness. How exactly did Jesus receive power? He responded to the temptations of Satan with "It is written." Christ knew and obeyed the *established* will of God. However, the enemy countered by also using scriptures. At that point Jesus responded with "It is said." He knew and obeyed the *communicated* will of God (see Luke 4:9-12).

We think of warfare in terms of "binding and loosing," but the endorsement of heaven, which actually accomplishes what we have decreed, is established in the wilderness of temptation and weakness. There is no authority without Christlike character; no lasting deliverance without facing the enemy and defeating him with God's Word.

Jesus lived by every word that proceeded out of the mouth of God, both written and spoken. In the overall strategy of God, this is central to His plans: that the church, first of all, become Christlike. When we feel tempted and self-condemned, we must remember it is here, in this season of weakness, that character is developed and anointed power comes to deliver us from the devil.

Blessed Father, You are our strategy; You are our power. Grant us courage to overcome the enemy in spite of our weaknesses. For the sake of the multitudes who will experience Your anointed power upon us, grant us victory to obey You even when no one is looking. In Jesus' name, amen.

TWENTY-ONE

It Takes a Citywide Church

*M*any Christians believe that in the last days the only unity will be in the apostate church. Ironically, it is the very enemy they fear, the antichrist, that has separated them from other born-again churches in their city! Their aloofness is rooted in self-righteousness. Such an attitude cannot win the war for their cities!

United in Worship and War

One need not be a Bible scholar to recognize that the Jews had to be uncompromisingly united in their worship of God. All Israel was required to come to Jerusalem three times a year to worship during the feasts. If their worship was compromised, and they were serving the pagan gods of the region, they could not stand in battle. However, in addition to unity in worship, they also had to be united in warfare. Unless they ultimately faced the battle as "one man," their victory was rarely assured. (See Judg. 6:16; 20:1,8,11; 1 Sam. 11:7; Ezra 3:1.)

From the beginning, the Lord has called us to be our brother's keeper. His standard has not changed. Today He is still calling us to cease fighting with one another and to unite in Christ against our common enemies.

There is an Old Testament story which reveals the heart we are seeking. The Israelites were in the land of Gilead about to cross the Jordan River (Num. 32). The tribes of Reuben and Gad, which had amassed much livestock, asked that their inheritance be given first, as the land on which they stood was suitable for grazing. Their request angered Moses for he assumed they sought to divide from the nation in order to gain their individual inheritance.

However, Reuben and Gad had a vision greater than Moses realized. Their words to Moses capture the attitude we must have concerning the other churches in our cities. They said, "We will build here sheepfolds for our livestock and cities for our little ones; but we ourselves will be armed ready to go before the sons of Israel, until we have brought them to their place" (Num. 32:16,17). They refused to put down their swords until every tribe had gained its inheritance.

Truly, each church must maintain its individual "sheepfolds," the local fellowship, for the sense of family and continuity. We are compelled by God's love to provide a spiritual shelter to raise our "little ones." However, we must also be armed and ready to war on behalf of our brethren.

You see, although we are divided by "tribes" (denominations), we are all part of the same spiritual nation. And while we all have unique battles facing us, our collective and conscious unity under Christ's anointing brings terror to the heart of our enemy. It is this united house of the Lord that will turn our cities to God.

Consequently, in this hour God is raising up strong, seasoned leaders who are equipping their saints to pray and war in behalf of the *other* churches in their city. Intercessors are being trained, not only to protect and defend the citywide church, but to go before them to help secure their inheritance in Christ. Our prayer is that the attitude in Reuben and Gad will become the stance of the mature churches in every city. They said, "We will not return to our homes until every one of the sons of Israel has possessed his inheritance" (Num. 32:18).

Our Strategy in Spiritual Warfare

To go successfully before our brethren in war, the Lord Himself must prepare us. If we ignore the Lord's training, a confrontational posture against the enemy will be, at best, ineffective and, at worst, dangerous. If you attempt to "bind" a principality or power but harbor sin in your heart, you will certainly be defeated. We have no authority over a foe *outside* of us if we are compromising with that foe *inside* of us. Thus, after discerning a ruling principality or power over an area, our first step in warfare is to cleanse the citywide church of its openness toward demonic influence. After pulling down the corresponding strongholds among the people, we then seek God in order to discern if this is an enemy He is calling us to confront.

When we were in the Washington, D.C., area, the Lord revealed that we were to pray against the power of deceit over the area. Since deceit was also somewhat operative in the church, our first act was to cleanse the participating congregation of deception. We did so by calling everyone to expose and confess their secret sins. After breaking the power of deceit over us, we prayed. That very evening, Marion Barry, the mayor of Washington, was arrested for drug use. The media reported that the police had sought his arrest for years, but he had cloaked himself in deceit.

As in any war, many things must be in place before the Lord will engage the church in confrontational warfare. We must not be anxious to try our new "doctrinal gun" of spiritual warfare, especially if our hearts are not filled with the fire-power of Christ Himself.

More often, however, the Lord gives discernment, not for us to engage in warfare, but so that we will be aware of the enemy and be cleansed of his influence. In the initial stages of our training, we will soon discover that the Lord is more concerned with establishing His presence in the church than He is with addressing the regional principalities and powers. For it is not until the nature of Christ is in us, and the voice of Christ is speaking through us, that the Spirit of Christ penetrates the heavenly places, displacing the spiritual darkness over an area.

Suppose, however, that a number of churches are participating and that you have repented and are cleansed of the influence of the specific enemy you seek to confront. How do you engage in warfare? The answer to this question is multifaceted. First, our prayers must be scripturally based expressions of God's *written* judgment as seen in the Scriptures. The "sword of the Spirit" is the "word of God" (Eph. 6:17). We must never boast about what we will do to the devil. We are servants carrying out God's will through speaking His Word.

Additionally, our prayers are not mere words without corresponding actions. Our prayer of judgment is a representation of our commitment to see the kingdom of God prevail in the very territory Satan held, even if it costs us our lives. In other words, our prayers are backed up by a willingness to die for what we believe.

Prayer is not our only weapon. Our feet are shod in preparation to speak the gospel. While we war in prayer, we are simultaneously reaching out to people through evangelism, seminars and publications; through teaching on the radio and television; and, when appropriate, by participating in public demonstrations. You see, although our assault begins in the heavenly places, it extends to many fronts.

"By My Spirit," Says the Lord

Jesus said, "If I cast out demons by the Spirit of God, then the kingdom of God has come upon you" (Matt. 12:28). The actual practice of waging spiritual war must be accomplished through the Holy Spirit. Jesus said the Spirit would "convict the world concerning sin, and righteousness, and judgment" (John 16:8). As individuals, the path of spiritual maturity begins with conviction of sin. It leads to our receiving Christ Himself as our righteousness. As Christ dwells within us, judgment is manifested against the enemy.

We must see that it is Christ in us who initiates our war against hell. Those who warn against immature Christians engaging in spiritual warfare are correct. To succeed, we must wage a *holy* war. As we have participated with the Holy Spirit in the transformation of our souls, so also are we joined with Him as He leads us into confrontational warfare. By this He manifests the word of divine judgment against "the ruler of this world" (John 16:11).

Please also note that Jesus said the Spirit would convict the world concerning sin. This is important. Judgment begins first with the household of God. However, the same Holy Spirit who has transformed us enlists us to transform society. And in His war against the devil, the same pattern which captured us is used against the world. Thus, the Holy Spirit brings conviction to a city; He establishes righteous attitudes in the soul of that city; and to the degree the community turns toward God, Satan is displaced in the heavenly places.

Therefore, as we discern the strongholds over our cities, we ask the Spirit to bring conviction to our society concerning these specific sins. During one of our city prayer times, we prayed that the Holy Spirit would convict drug dealers of sin. We even asked that He would make them fearful, so they would come tearfully to God for help. A few days later I received a call from a man who had been selling drugs. He was crying, desperate and scared. He reported that a number of drug dealers in the city had similar feelings; some had even decided to take financial losses and leave. He himself had been a Christian and was backslidden. Today this man is a thankful member of our congregation. Now when he cries, his tears are tears of joy at the wonderful mercies of God.

Along with divine conviction of sin, we pray that the Holy Spirit would bring righteousness into the thoughts and attitudes of the secular leaders. We intercede for governmental agencies to judge and act with righteous judgments, praying for specific individuals to come to know Christ. We pray the same way for the newspaper and local television. In that regard, we have seen the paper swing toward a more conservative profile. In an editorial they actually commended an anti-satanism demonstration we held in a downtown park on Halloween. Do not just lament the condition of the communications media; intercede for them, praying that the Holy Spirit would convict them of sin and inspire righteousness in their attitudes.

The third phase or arena of warfare the Holy Spirit engages in is judgment: "because the ruler of this world has been judged" (John 16:11). It is part of the Holy Spirit's ministry to bring God's judgment against demons, principalities and powers. Satan has already been disarmed and rendered powerless, defeated at the cross of Christ (see Col. 2:15; Heb. 2:14; 1 John 3:8). The Holy Spirit conveys this eternal reality, granting authority to the church to establish God's will on earth as it is in heaven.

Some churches in our city have come together as a result of our war against the spirit of antichrist. The antichrist spirit divides Christians over minor doctrinal issues. One of the pastors with whom we pray felt the Lord wanted to bring healing between the Pentecostals and Baptists in town. Following his lead, we repented of spiritual pride concerning the gift of tongues, asking God to direct us to our Baptist friends.

That very evening, as I was looking for a used computer to purchase, I called a classified ad in the paper. Although the man who had placed the ad introduced himself as a Baptist pastor, I had forgotten our prayer. The following morning I went to his house. After an hour or so of computer talk, I stood to leave.

Suddenly, the Baptist pastor asked, "What is God doing?"

I finally remembered our prayer! Tears filled my eyes as the presence of the Lord entered the room. I told him that, just the day before, we had asked God to lead us, and that as charismatics and Pentecostals we had repented for allowing the gifts of the Spirit to divide us from other Christians.

"Wait!" he exclaimed. "I was just with the Baptist pastors in town telling them how we needed more of the gifts of the Spirit like the Pentecostals!"

The next week this pastor was united with us in prayer, and two weeks later we were praying with him at his church. In time he brought another Baptist pastor, a wonderful brother, into the prayer fellowship. It is significant that the first pastor's name is Paul Widen, for we feel God surely wants to widen our vision of the church.

This is the ministry of the Holy Spirit. Our warfare is never to be fought with human might or natural power. Only as the Spirit of the Lord works with us do we see the church rebuilt and victory come. God wants us directed into Spirit-led prayer that confronts the strongholds of the city, utilizing the power of the Holy Spirit as our weapon.

Dry Bones or a Great Army?

One obstacle we must overcome is the illusion that we, because of our ability to "divide the word," are more spiritual than other churches. This delusion works on many churches concurrently and separates congregations throughout a city. Thus, we remain divided, isolated by our own spiritual pride. But, as God delivers us from our arrogance, we see that we are without understanding when we compare ourselves to ourselves. We are not called to judge one another but to "love one another."

What God is doing today is much like the restoration of the Jews from their Babylonian captivity. Under the threat of warfare, and in spite of discouragement, the Jews were rebuilding the temple. Nehemiah instructed the workers to carry a building tool in one hand and a sword in the other (see Neh. 4:17). If one section of the wall came under attack, a trumpet sounded, and all rallied to defend that area.

It must be the same for us. Many times the enemy has been able to defeat a particular church only because the rest of the citywide church was indifferent or unaware of the battle. In this context we must perceive that it takes a citywide church to win the citywide war.

I hear the reply: "The churches in our city are dead, and we alone are left." Such was Elijah's lament, but the Lord assured him there were yet seven thousand who were faithful. Ezekiel also thought he stood alone, but God brought him out to a valley of dry bones and commanded him to prophesy, to speak to those bones. *After* the bones came together, then the Spirit entered; and, behold, they were "an exceedingly great army" (Ezek. 37:10b).

One of the sins of the church is that we criticize the dry bones, judging them for being lifeless. Yet we fail simply to *speak* to them. There are thousands of pastors and churches that only need to be spoken to and connected with others in the body. God is indeed preparing an exceedingly great army. Through it He intends to pull down the strongholds in the cities. However, they must be *connected in Christ* before the Spirit will anoint them for effective spiritual warfare.

Please hear me. We are fully supportive. We thank God for national days of prayer and regional weeks of supplication, and we are calling tens of thousands to pray for specific areas to change. These strategies are essential for loosening the enemy's grip over an area. But if we want to see Satan's kingdom fall, the church must be united. For if the city church is bound and divided by strife, the enemy in that region will not be plundered.

When we pray against the spiritual forces of wickedness over a region, our first line of offense is to pray for the churches to be united in their worship and their warfare. Why pray for the church? The Scriptures tell us that "the adversary and the enemy entered the gates of the city because of the sins of the prophets and the iniquities of the priests" (Lam. 4:16-17). Indeed, if "there is jealousy and selfish ambition" in the church, there will inevitably be "disorder and every evil thing" in that locality (James 3:16).

Therefore, we conclude: It takes a citywide church to win the citywide war. Our individual evangelistic programs, our Sunday teachings and our aggressive attempts to bind the enemy are of limited value if we, the born-again church, remain divided. One person's transformation from carnality to the image of Christ can revolutionize a church; the transformation of the citywide church into the image of Christ can revolutionize a city.

Let's pray.

Lord Jesus, forgive me for being so independent that I failed to see the needs of the other churches in my city. You said that a house divided cannot stand. You also said that if we are not gathering with You in spiritual warfare, we are actually against You. Lord, I repent of being isolated. I ask You to equip me to be a strength and a help to my brethren throughout the city. Grant me grace, Lord Jesus, to fulfill this prayer to Your glory. Amen.

TWENTY-TWO

Our Authority
in Christ

*M*any saints wonder whether Christians have the authority to pray against principalities and powers. The scriptural position is that we not only have the authority to war against
these spiritual enemies, but we have the responsibility to do so!
As God leads us, we must pray against them, or they will, indeed,
prey upon us.

Our Model Is Jesus

In understanding the role and authority of the church in spiritual
warfare, we have no other example than Jesus. The Bible tells us that
"we are to grow up into all aspects into Him, who is the head, even
Christ" (Eph. 4:15). The direction of the church is always toward

Christlikeness. Thus, only by studying Jesus Himself with a view toward our own personal transformation will the mystery of the church be solved and the purpose of God be accomplished. For the anointing and nature of Christ *are* the call and destiny of the church.

Knowing, therefore, the Father's eternal plan to make man in Christ's image, the Son of God Himself confidently assures us: "He who believes in Me, the works that I do shall he do also" (John 14:12). John also connects the nature of Christ with the authority and purpose of the church. He wrote, "As He is, so also are we in this world" (1 John 4:17). If we truly desire heaven's endorsement, then our doctrines and objectives must be built upon this one foundation: Truth is in Jesus.

Therefore, let us ask ourselves: Are we doing what Jesus did? For whatever Jesus did, the Spirit-anointed church will do likewise. Did Jesus love? Then those who serve Him will love with His love. Did He pray? Then His disciples will pray with His fervor. And if Christ engaged in spiritual warfare, it follows that His body will also wage war.

Jesus obviously confronted unclean spirits that were resident in the physical and spiritual nature of man. These entities were not simply inherent psychological weaknesses; they were demons. Whether it was the Gerasene demoniac with many demons or the more usual deliverance of one or two spirits, Jesus certainly waged spiritual warfare (see Matt. 8:28-34). And if Jesus cast out demons, then we should expect His disciples to do likewise, for of His fullness we have all received (see John 1:16).

Even a casual observer can see that Jesus had an attitude of war toward Satan. In fact, all that He did, whether loving, healing, teaching, even the simple act of blessing children, was involved in destroying the works of Satan.

Jesus also aggressively *pursued* His enemies. For whenever Jesus perceived hell's evil workers, He confronted them in His authority— and He did so without fear or the slightest hesitation. Even with the Gerasene demoniac, who was violently insane and supernaturally powerful, Christ fearlessly and immediately engaged Himself in warfare with the man's tormentors.

Furthermore, knowing the ongoing state of war which would exist after He left, we see Jesus building a church to prevail against the gates of hell. Jesus sent forth His disciples, instructing them to cast out demons and giving them "authority...over all the power of the enemy" (see Matt. 16:18; Luke 10:19; 9:1).

Remember, our model is none other than Jesus. Not only did He live without fear, but demons were terrified of Him! He was never presumptuous, yet just His gaze flooded evil spirits with trembling and torment. Consider: Christ's promise to everyone who believes in Him is that "greater works than these shall [you] do; because I go unto the Father" (John 14:12).

Christ and Principalities and Powers

The question arises, But did Jesus confront principalities and powers? We have no Gospel account of His challenging the ruling powers over Israel. In fact, we find no mention of the word "principality" in any of Christ's discourses. However, He is apparently speaking with reference to both principalities and powers in Matthew 24:29, where He states that before He returns "the powers of the heavens will be shaken."

Although we do not find scriptural examples of His addressing evil powers as such, the above question might be better rephrased to ask: Did Jesus confront the kingdom of darkness on any level higher than demonic possession? Yes, Jesus clashed with the prince of darkness, Satan himself.

Christ's war was even beyond the territorial battle associated with principalities and powers. Although regionally located, His spiritual warfare was global in consequence. He did not come merely to redeem a city or a nation but the world. The fact is that, when the Prince of Peace came, the prince of darkness rose to meet Him: Satan was Jesus' adversary.

New Levels, New Devils

As I see it, there is a type of order to spiritual warfare. Satan himself does not attack new Christians, nor does the Lord require new Christians to attack the type of principalities or powers that rule over nations and certain ethnic and religious groups. Satan, the former archangel, does not have to attack Christians personally when a minor demon can sidetrack most of us.

Contrary to what we may have thought, Lucifer, as he was formerly called, rarely attacks individuals. In my opinion, there are probably fewer than forty individuals in today's world who are actually considered a threat and worthy of his focused, steadfast attention. It would be safe to say that most spiritual warfare is an exercise in authority over demons. Few Christians will be called to confront the highest level of principalities and powers.

Evil spirits are assigned against us proportionately, according to the threat we may pose to hell. With each new spiritual level attained there is a fiercer, more adept enemy awaiting us. And while only some might actually face Satan himself, many in the church today are being trained and anointed to mobilize the church and defeat the ruling evil spirits in their regions.

In the first century Christ's apostles were of such a stature that they actually became a threat not only to principalities and powers, but to the devil himself. In response to their personal confrontations with Satan, they unhesitatingly wrote their warnings in the Scriptures and also gave instructions on how to overcome.

It should be noted that, when the Scriptures speak specifically about the devil, the usual inference is that the writer is referring to the more typical battle against an evil spirit and not the devil himself. The precepts they applied against Satan work with every level of demonic attack, whether a principality or power, a demon or an imp.

From his own confrontations with Satan, for example, Peter speaks of the devil as a "roaring lion, seeking someone to devour." Yet he said to remain "firm in the faith," and God will supply the power to "resist" him (1 Pet. 5:8-9). James also speaks of spiritual warfare.

From his experience with spiritual attacks he writes, "Submit therefore to God. Resist the devil and he will flee from you" (James 4:7). You, as a new creation in Christ, have the power to resist the devil. Out of your submission to Christ, Satan will actually flee from you!

In speaking to the young men in the church, the apostle John wrote, "You are strong and the word of God abides in you, and you have overcome the evil one" (1 John 2:14). He reminds us that Jesus came to "destroy the works of the devil" (1 John 3:8). John goes so far as to say that "greater is He who is in us than he who is in the world" (1 John 4:4) and that there is a place of hiddenness in Christ where the evil one cannot touch us at all.

The Church at God's Throne

So we see that Jesus exercised authority over all the power of the enemy and that He gave this same authority to the church. It is our task to follow Him. Every pastor needs to know when a situation calls for counseling and encouragement or when a demonic stronghold must be confronted and spiritual authority exercised. For more information on this subject we suggest reading *The Three Battlegrounds* by this author.

Because of the increasing battle at the end of this age, each one of us should know the scriptural basis of our authority in Christ. Paul wrote, "I pray that the eyes of your heart may be enlightened, so that you may know what is the hope of His calling, what are the riches of the glory of His inheritance in the saints, and what is the surpassing greatness of His power toward us who believe" (Eph. 1:18-19).

Through your faith in God there is a divine power being directed toward you, even now as you read this . Paul says this power is *the very same power* which resurrected Jesus, "which He brought about in Christ, when He raised Him from the dead, and seated Him at His right hand in the heavenly places, far above all rule and authority and power and dominion" (Eph. 1:20-21).

All true Christians believe Jesus Christ is Lord and that He is seated

157

at the right hand of God. Theologically we are in agreement about Christ's positional authority. What we fail to see is *our* authority as Christ's body and His agents upon earth. Paul continues, "And He put all things in subjection under His feet, and gave him as head over all things to the church, which is His body, the fullness of Him who fills all in all" (Eph. 1:22-23).

Notice three key words: *feet, head* and *body*. Jesus is head of a body which has feet; under His feet all things have been put in subjection. The Holy Spirit is not limiting the subjection of all things to be under Christ's physical feet at the throne of God. No! The context is plain: Christ is head over a *body* (1 Cor. 12:12); all things are under the *feet* of that body. The "feet" are those members which walk upon the earth.

The feet do not have one authority and the head another; rather as long as the feet are in subjection to the head and carrying out His will, their authority *is* the expansion of His authority. Notice also that the "things in subjection" include by name principalities and powers. Note also that this phrase "in subjection" is a military term, speaking of the victor's authority over the vanquished.

Paul is stating here that through the yielded, obedient church the authority of Jesus is exhibited in militant and triumphant victory over all the power of the devil, even over principalities and powers in the heavenly places. No wonder Paul began this discourse by saying, "I pray that the eyes of your heart may be enlightened" (Eph. 1:18).

The typical self-concept of church members is earthly in nature. However, Paul tells us that there is another dimension to "new creation" people. He says that God "raised us up and seated us with Him in the heavenly places in Christ Jesus." Jesus does not have one seat next to the Father and another seat next to us in the heavenly places. The "heavenly places seat" and God's "right hand seat" are the same place. He has raised us up and seated us with Him far above all rule and authority and power and dominion.

Right now, spiritually and positionally, through the redemptive life of Christ, we are part of an army which is at the same time both earthly and heavenly in nature. The fact is, if Christ is truly with us here, then we are indeed with Him there. For Christ and His church are one.

The Father's Promise to His Son

Psalm 110:1 documents a most amazing conversation. We discover in this text a promise spoken from the Father directly to His Son. It reads, "The Lord says to my Lord: 'Sit at My right hand, until I make Thine enemies a footstool for Thy feet.' " God the Father is set upon making Christ's enemies a footstool for His feet. We are not learning about warfare because we, on our own initiative, decided to learn it. God Himself has chosen to equip us to fulfill His promise to His Son.

In effect the Father said to His Son, "I resurrected You, bringing You through all eternity to seat You next to Me on My throne. Rest at My right hand. The Holy Spirit will unite You with those who believe. Spiritually, they will actually become Your body; those living on the earth will become as Your feet. As the God of peace, I will crush Satan beneath Your 'feet' " (Rom. 16:20).

Psalm 110 is the Old Testament passage that supported Paul's revelation to the Ephesians. The very same power God used to raise Jesus is now training us to tread upon serpents and scorpions and is giving us authority over all the power of the enemy (see Luke 10:18-19). We have been granted this authority as a fulfillment of the promise between the Father and His Son.

The Voice of God

We must learn to use the authority of Christ, not presumptuously, but administratively and compassionately. For there is an unparalleled spiritual assault against cities and our children by the enemy. Yet the weapons of our warfare are mighty. Additionally, the Lord Himself is shaking the powers of darkness in the heavenly places.

"On that day the Lord will punish the fallen angels in the heavens, and the proud rulers of the nations on earth" (Is. 24:21, LB). While we are seeing with our own eyes the beginnings of the Lord's punishment of the proud rulers of the nations, especially in the communist countries, we do not see the Lord's punishment of the "fallen angels in the heavens." He is toppling the principalities and powers whose influence seemed unshakeable.

At the end of the age the Lord has promised a shaking that will topple all things. We read in Hebrews that "He has promised, saying, 'Yet once more I will shake not only the earth, but also the heaven' " (Heb. 12:26).

The "heaven" to which this text refers is the heavenly places, the spiritual realm which immediately surrounds the earth. This text tells us that prior to His return the Lord will speak a word which will shake and cleanse even the spirit realm surrounding our world. Hebrews continues, "This expression, 'Yet once more,' denotes the removing of those things which can be shaken, as of created things, in order that those things which cannot be shaken may remain. Therefore, since we receive a kingdom which cannot be shaken, let us show gratitude" (Heb. 12:27-29).

God is going to remove the proud rulers of the earth and the demonic rulers from the heavenlies. He is doing it right before our eyes. As the wrestling continues between the church and the hosts of hell, we are beginning to learn the enemy's moves.

We know how to submit to God and resist the devil, and we can discern the "accuser of the brethren." We have learned to anticipate and protect ourselves against temptation, to stand in spite of fear and to persevere even while we are weary. And knowing that every demon is a liar, we know not to listen or believe the voice of our adversary.

We also are learning the Lord's "moves." We know Christ's humility is our armor, His love is our strength, and His forgiveness disarms demons. We know the power of the blood, the authority of Jesus' name and the importance of our testimony. We are no longer ignorant of Satan's devices. We know it is our eternal destiny to win this war!

God has something to say to the "authorities in the heavenly places." And it is the wisdom of God that *the church*, the once-fallen but now cleansed and redeemed church, should be His vehicle to complete His judgment of the devil.

For those who question the timing of all this, Paul tells us that this ministry of God is not just "in the age to come" but "now...through the church to the rulers and the authorities" (Eph. 3:10; see also Eph. 1:21). The first-century church was an instrument of God unto principalities and powers. So also will the last earthly church be used by God in spiritual warfare.

TWENTY-THREE

The Battle
After a
Breakthrough

T here will be a battle after every breakthrough in God. That battle will be centered upon one main front: the Word! Will we believe the Word during the time of testing, or will we fall back to our former state of unbelief and bondage?

In this chapter we want to expose one avenue of assault that comes against the church especially following a major breakthrough or a citywide warfare conference. The area of battle to which we refer is the testing ground of our words.

Predictably, after a large gathering of pastors and churches, much of the conversation is electrified with memories of recent events: People and churches are delivered of demonic activity, strongholds are pulled down, and the enemy is exposed. The goal of Christlikeness is made clear, and grace is present to make it attainable. A new day seemingly breaks upon a city, and there is much to discuss and rejoice over. Yet in the midst of our excitement we must remember: We have only witnessed a beginning. Not only will we be judged for every idle or careless word we speak, but every word of God is tested also (see Matt. 12:36; Ps. 105:19). Our words must be backed by *substance* and *character* before we will see the purposes of God fully established.

You will remember that Jesus, after being baptized by John, was confirmed as God's Son by the divine utterance of the Father Himself, "This is My beloved Son" (Matt. 3:17). Yet the plan of God was that Jesus be led not into "the ministry" but into spiritual conflict. The same Spirit who descended and rested gently like a dove upon Christ now drove Him into the desert. Suddenly Jesus found Himself facing Satan in intense spiritual warfare. The issue of the conflict was the very word Christ had just received from God at His baptism; the challenge from the enemy was, "*If* you are the Son of God" (Matt. 4:3).

Whenever a word from the Lord is spoken, expect that it will be contested by the devil. The battle will, without fail, be fought over what God has said. In the Garden of Eden it was so, with Christ in the wilderness it was so, and thus it will be for us as well. This battle will not be won merely with the procedure of "binding" and "loosing." It will be won with *Christlike character* and holding fast to the word God has spoken.

Throughout the battle we must not back off either from our vision or from our faith, for it is our destiny to triumph in Christ! However, the issues here are not centered upon developing our spiritual authority but our *loyalty* to the Father during trial. Christ overcame the devil by His purity and devotion to God. Not until He passed this test did He receive divine power to fulfill the word which was spoken (Luke 4:14).

Today through many individuals the Spirit of God is speaking a pure word for the church concerning the house of the Lord and doing spiritual warfare. However, before we will walk in what is spoken, God will allow Satan to test us. If church leaders make a statement such as "Now we have a citywide church," or "The enemy was finally defeated," the devil will have an open door to discourage and then frustrate their faith. Our only answer in this assault is that our words must be backed up by functional Christlikeness.

We must not be afraid of this satanic counterattack. It is almost inevitable. When rightly interpreted it is an encouragement to us, a sign that we have been effectively hitting the enemy. Yet we must also learn from this assault that wherever our words and declarations are incomplete or halfhearted, these will become the new targets of satanic assault.

It is vital that we discern this counterattack correctly. We must allow God to make the battleground of our failings the next area where Christlike transformation is worked in us. Satan seeks to exploit our weaknesses; God seeks to establish, in the very area of our weaknesses, the nature of His Son. All things must be perceived and understood in light of this reality.

In time we will realize it is wisdom to keep our declarations of recent spiritual achievements low-key. Jesus knew He was the Son of God, yet He referred to Himself most frequently as the Son of Man. He let others confirm by the Spirit what could come only by revelation, and so must we. Without sacrificing the boldness of our faith nor entering into false humility, our confession must be without exaggeration or presumptuous statements. This move of God is His work. He will promote it with power. Let our confession be: "We have had a breakthrough; now let us humbly seek the Almighty to sustain it." Remember, every area where we are not Christlike will become an area of warfare, even to the testing of our confession and in the simple relating of facts.

One Last Thing

Many of you have been committed to building the house of the Lord and dealing with the spiritual warfare that it involves. However, the enemy will seek to dilute your vision with distractions such as family commitments during holiday seasons, vacations and so forth. These natural and honorable events of our lives can easily become occasions where the passion for the purposes of God wanes. Attendance in prayer meetings will inevitably fluctuate with the increase or decrease of these factors.

Simultaneously, lower attendance at prayer meetings will be used by the enemy to discourage even the most faithful from the position of prayer. If we have such a setback, we must not interpret it to mean that the Lord is leading us to curtail intercession. Both your church and your city are being protected by prayer. While we may make procedural and seasonal adjustments, we must not put down the sword.

Daniel records an amazing vision which is relevant to our battles. "I kept looking, and that horn was waging war with the saints and overpowering them until the Ancient of Days came, and judgment was passed in favor of the saints of the Highest One, and the time arrived when the saints took possession of the kingdom" (Dan. 7:21-22).

Daniel's vision should remind us that whenever warfare is initiated, a time of struggle will follow when it seems as though we are being overpowered. However, we must stand firm in the midst of this battle. While we continue to stand, and as Christlike character is worked within us, judgment will be passed in favor of the saints.

Remember: There is always a battle after a breakthrough. But as you hold fast to the Word, and as we fix our minds upon Christ, the time will arrive when we will sustain our breakthrough and hold the land. Our cities will be established under the influence of God!

CONCLUSION

*W*e have stated throughout this book that there is a resolution to our present distress, but that the answer lies in the bosom of the church and in the context of our doing the will of God. The following is a summary of what we are convinced is the only hope for any city or nation during these times. Our prayer is that you will hear God's heart for yourself and, joined with others of like vision, will help build the house of the Lord.

Here is a brief overview of our situation and the answers we believe God has given.

The Problems

1. Evil is increasing in cities throughout the country

2. Government is spending billions; little or nothing is working.

3. The number of practicing Christians, in general, has not increased in North America.

4. Most born-again Christians have a limited revelation of the harvest; most do not understand their authority to protect their city, and they are somewhat ignorant of the provisions of God.

5. While the only earthly channel God can use to touch the nation is the body of Christ, the church has been, with a few exceptions, weak in dealing with the problems of society.

Considerations

1. There is only one hope for turning our nation around; that hope is the obedient, united, Christ-centered church.

2. This process of renewal must be accomplished city by city, church by church and person by person.

3. The church in its divided state cannot stand against its enemies.

4. Jesus Himself wants our cities and has initiated His strategy to use the church. Unity is essential, but unity without Jesus is worthless. The power and authority of the church are not in its unity but in its relationship with Jesus.

Strategy

1. Establish in the church its true purpose, which is Christlikeness. Doctrines which do not support transformation are given a lesser priority. Focus is riveted upon Christ in the Gospels.

2. Cleanse the church of its visionless and loveless relationship to its city. Nineveh repented. Jesus said if His miracles were done in Sodom it would have repented. In many instances a righteous judge or king arose and turned all Israel back to God. To pray and see entire cities returned to the Lord is both scriptural and possible.

3. Discern the specific satanic strongholds in the region. Through repentance and faith in God's ability these strongholds must be removed. (See *The Three Battlegrounds* by this author and *Taking Our Cities for God* by John Dawson.)

4. Once satanic strongholds are pulled down in the church through repentance, the church has authority to war effectively against evil.

5. Position the church in daily prayer and spiritual warfare in a minimum of five different church locations throughout the city. Members of various congregations meet in each location.

Commitment

This call requires the laying down of our lives to see the will of God fulfilled. We encourage the reader to receive from God the grace necessary to make the following commitments.

1. Only where the pastors and churches have overcome pride and ambition is there grace enough to change an entire city. Therefore with God's help I commit myself to uniting with other pastors, intercessors and believers for the purpose of prayer and action for our city.

2. Only persevering prayer will prove worthy to launch revival. Therefore I commit myself to faithfulness in prayer, pledging myself to corporate prayer with other pastors and intercessors once a week, ultimately expanding that to praying every day.

3. Since the answer for every battle is more of Jesus in the church, our goal must be to see Jesus glorified in our lives. Therefore I commit myself to a life of surrender, that He might increase through me into the world.

Dear Lord, You deserve our hearts, our churches and our cities. Forgive us for being distracted by the world and our ambitions. Lord, by Your grace we commit ourselves to Your purposes, that our lives will be qualitatively capable of becoming Your house, and our words will be worthy of the endorsement of Your power. In Jesus' name, amen.

GLOSSARY

Demons, devils: Greek: *daimon,* demons. King James wrongly translates "demons" as "devils." There are two separate words translated "devil" in the New Testament, each representing a different spiritual entity. There is only one devil, Satan, but there are many demons. Demons were once angels "who left their first estate" (Jude 6; Rev. 12:9; Matt. 25:41).

These spiritual entities differ in degrees of wickedness (Matt. 12:45). Everything from impish little spirits to major principalities and powers can be categorized as demons when the term is used generally. However, when "demon" is used as a specific reference, it usually speaks of any number of unclean spirits, such as deaf and dumb spirits, spirits of fear, lust and so forth, which masquerade as human thoughts.

Demons are the "ground troops" of hell. They are the most abundant of evil spirits, and evidently God has given them a "legal" right to occupy any territory that exists in defiant rebellion to His will, including mankind. Jude 6 tells us that these fallen angels are kept in eternal bonds of darkness, which is a spiritual place of moral depravity. The responsibility to "cast out demons" belongs to all believers (Mark 16:17).

Devil: Greek: *diabolos,* an accuser, a slanderer. One of the identities of Satan. From this word the English word "devil" is derived and should be applied only to Satan (Vine's Expository Dictionary). (See "Satan," below)

Heavenly places: When the Scriptures refer to heaven, they may be speaking of any of three places which the context of the reference

171

interprets. The "first heaven" is the celestial heaven: the sun, moon and stars (Ps. 19:1). The "third heaven" is perhaps the most familiar definition; it is the first of many levels of glory, known also as "paradise" (2 Cor. 12:2,4), which is crowned by the highest of heavens, the dwelling place of God (Matt. 6:9).

Finally, there is the realm known in the Scriptures as the "heavenly places." It is this realm which is the battleground of our spiritual warfare. It is here that good and evil spirits clash in the battle for men's souls. Ultimately, when the Lord Jesus returns and all evil is banished, this heaven will be filled with the glory of God. (See Eph. 3:10; 6:12.)

House of the Lord: In a universal and true sense, every Christian is part of the Lord's eternal house. Practically speaking, however, the house of the Lord is only functional as we are "built together," where the church becomes "a dwelling of God in the Spirit" (Eph. 2:19-22). Therefore, we have taken a liberty in this book to define the house of the Lord as that living, united, praying church in the city. The Lord's house will consist of evangelicals and Pentecostals, traditional churches and charismatics; it will be free of racial and class prejudices. They will simply be Christians who know Jesus as Lord, believe the truth of the Scriptures and are committed to one another as brethren. Although they will continue to maintain their national affiliations, they will be uniquely anointed to bring healing to their cities.

Kingdom of God: Scripturally speaking, this phrase always refers to the eternal spiritual reality where the rule of God through Christ originates. The expanse of this heavenly kingdom has two primary manifestations: heaven in eternity, and the *fragrance* of heaven in the realm of time, which is revealed and entered through Christ. When this author speaks of "establishing the kingdom," it is in context with the latter definition. It is not our view that the whole earth must be subdued and made subject to Christ before He returns. Rather we speak of the kingdom of God as that dimension of eternal life which the redeemed inherit through spiritual rebirth and which the obedient discover in the meaning of Christ's words. (See Mark 1:14-15; Matt. 5:3,10; 6:33; and others.)

Powers: Working with principalities but in subjection to them are what the Bible calls "powers." The energy of a power is beamed outward from itself, broadcast like radio waves, over the territory. A power is a major demonic spirit whose primary activity is to blanket a given area with the energy of its particular evil. They are called "powers" because that is what they are: powers of darkness. They are the evil counterparts of the angelic class *virtues*. A church may have several particular virtues ministering through it, such as joy or faith, the same way a power of fear or depression may minister through a certain degenerate section of town.

Powers occupy a jurisdiction that is often county-wide, although a power may frequent the mind of an influential person or build a certain negative attitude within a church. Major powers also influence the spirit realm over entire regions of countries. Different powers will work together under the control of a principality, but usually one or two will be the most influential, eventually affecting even the mannerisms of speech in that area. (Compare the hard dialect of the states surrounding New York City with the slower, almost dallying language of sectors of the South.)

As is the case with principalities, the means through which the church successfully wars against powers is the administration of Christ's spiritual authority and the principle of displacement. Powers are not "cast out"; they are *displaced* in the spirit realm by the fullness of the reign of Christ in the church and through the intercessory warfare of the saints in the region. (See Matt. 24:29; Eph. 3:10; 6:12.)

Principality: Greek: *arche*. The word means "beginning, government, rule" and is used to describe a class of spirit beings in the satanic hierarchy. Principalities rule over powers as well as the more numerous subcategories of demons. Principalities influence countries, regions within countries, states, cities and even churches. These are governmental spirits in the system of hell and are the spiritual counterparts of archangels in heaven. They issue assignments and direct local warfare against the church. In general, they are the "administrators of evil" throughout any given area.

The church successfully wars against principalities through

Christ's spiritual authority and the principle of displacement. Principalities are not "cast out," for they do not dwell in people; they dwell in "heavenly places." They are displaced in the spirit realm by the ascendancy of Christ in the church and, through the church, into the community. (See Eph. 3:10; 6:12.)

Satan: Greek: *satanas,* adversary, one who resists. The principal name of the devil. Satan is the slanderer of men to God and of God to men. His assault against humanity is to cause men to sin, thereby invoking the judgment of God against mankind. Our warfare against Satan is successful when we remain pure and invoke the judgment of God against the devil. One of the ministries of the Holy Spirit is to bring God's judgment against Satan (see John 16:11).

The devil is the ultimate source of deception and lies as well as acts of violence. Jesus said of Satan that he is a thief who came to "steal, kill and destroy." Satan is the tempter. He is also the accuser of the brethren. Scripture also calls him the prince of this world and the god of this age. This author believes that Satan himself does not appear and directly attack people in general, but that the devil reserves his assaults for the Lord's anointed (Job, Christ, Peter). Scripturally speaking, Satan was rebuked but not "cast out" in the manner of dealing with demons. The church successfully wars against Satan by submitting to God; living, speaking and holding fast to the Word of God; knowing the power of Christ's sacrificial blood; and living the crucified life (see Rev. 12:10-12).

World rulers of darkness: When the Bible speaks of the "world rulers of darkness," it is speaking with reference to a certain class of principalities, a spiritual entity that, on a national scale, governs other principalities as well as the powers under them. The scope of a world ruler's influence is worldwide.

In the book of Daniel, one such principality was known as the "prince over Persia." This particular ruler fought with the angel that was sent in answer to prayer. On the natural level, Cyrus was king of Persia, but in the spirit realm there was another ruler. Daniel's intercession, you will remember, was instrumental in obtaining from King Cyrus permission for the Jews to return and rebuild Jerusalem. In the spirit realm, however, the world ruler was resisting. Finally,

Michael, who was an archangel over Israel (equivalent to the class of world ruler), joined the original angel that was sent to Daniel and defeated the enemy. The influence of the world rulers, as well as the principalities and powers, can be observed in the differing temperaments and cultures of the European nations. (See Eph. 3:10; 6:12.)

CHAPTER HIGHLIGHTS

Preface

It will take a citywide church to win the citywide war. Our separate, isolated efforts will not stop the flood of increasing evil in our cities if we, as Christ's church, remain isolated from each other. (11)

We have taken the liberty in this book to define the house of the Lord as that living, united, praying church in the city. The Lord's house will consist of evangelicals and Pentecostals, traditional churches and charismatics; it will be free of racial and class prejudices. (11-12)

Like all rivers, the eternal river of life *avoids* mountains. Yet it flows naturally into valleys and plains. Before we will ever be truly prepared for the Lord Jesus, the mountain of our pride must come down. It is a fact worth noting that, in preparation for Christ, God placed John the Baptist in the Jordan Valley. This valley is actually the lowest place in the world. The Lord began His greatest work in the lowest place on earth. Indeed, all those whom the Lord will empower will pass through a valley of lowliness. (12)

God will give grace to the humble, and together they will bring a new purity to Christianity. They will speak with lasting credibility of Christ's forgiveness; they will be examples of His love toward one another. (12)

Chapter 1

Out of His desire to present a pure bride to His Son, the Father is purging the church of its sin. (17)

Through new and successive levels of purity, the house of the Lord will again see and reflect the glory of God. (18)

God initiated His plan to redeem the nation by consecrating the priests and cleansing the house of the Lord. (18)

Before the eternal One moves visibly in power, He moves invisibly in holiness. (18)

It is one thing for us to speak honestly with the Lord; it is quite another when He speaks without restraint to us. (19)

For us to become sensitive to divine realities we must live with the door of our hearts open. It is impossible to do the will of God otherwise. (19)

We can be assured that each step deeper into the Lord's presence will reveal areas in our hearts which need to be cleansed. (21)

Chapter 2

There are costs to attaining God's best. If we want to have His greatest provisions, we must yield to Him our greatest loves. (23)

Even as the Lord carefully chose the building site for the temple of stone, so He is looking at the landscape of our hearts, seeking to make us His temple of flesh. (23)

Abraham's faith told him they would both return, but it was his attitude of worship which enabled him to go up. (24)

To qualify for the house of the Lord, the first attitude we must possess is a worshipping heart; we must be willing to give to God what we love the most. (24)

Those whom God chooses as the building site of His house will give to God what they have loved the most. Within their yielding, worshipping hearts, He will build His house. (25)

Chapter 3

If we will gain God's greatest blessings, we must embrace His highest purpose. (27)

If our goal is anything other than becoming a home for Jesus, this truth will become another "wind of doctrine"; we will be blown off course again. Without the abiding fullness of Christ in the church we will have no more impact in the world than a political party, whose strength rests in numbers and not in God. (27)

We need to return to the simplicity and purity of devotion to Christ; and we desperately need divine intervention, or our nation will perish. (28)

We must abandon all hope of finding true spiritual success apart from dependent, steadfast faith in the Person and power of Christ. (28)

We cannot attain to the works of God unless we first become the workmanship of God. (29)

Until we see that the Father's highest purpose is to reveal in us the *nature* of Christ, we will not qualify for the *power* of Christ, which is God's full endorsement upon our lives. (29)

That is, we cannot see Christ corporately manifested in the church until we, as individuals, embrace true Christlikeness; nor can we plunder the heavenly places until we unite with other congregations as Christ's church. (29)

It is the eternal wisdom and purpose of God to reveal Christ "through the church"—not only to the world but to the "rulers and the authorities [principalities and powers] in the heavenly places" (Eph. 3:10). (29-30)

In battling for the soul of our cities and our nation, our victory is not in knowing how to command demons, but in knowing the commander Himself. (30)

We triumph in being rightly aligned with the supreme plan of God, which is to fill all things with Christ. (30)

If we want to obtain the endorsement of God upon our lives, Jesus must become as real to us as the world was when we were sinners. (30)

Chapter 4

When pure Christianity degenerates into divided camps of ambitious people, it literally destroys the harmony, power and blessing of the "temple of God." (32)

The living God is a God of order; He will not dwell in ruins! Because He is a God of love, He will work with us to rebuild, but He *will not* sanction our fallen condition with power. He will not lend credibility to our disorder. (32-33)

Building the house of God, the born-again, praying, loving, citywide church, is still Christ's highest priority. (33)

The path narrows for leadership until our only privilege is to become Christlike in everything. (34)

Consequently the disorder, lawlessness and "every evil thing" we see in our society are, at least in part, rooted in the soil of a misdirected and distracted church community. (34)

Over the years the world has seen many incredible ministries. However, the time of the incredible has passed; the hour for the credible is being established. (34)

Chapter 5

We have instructed the church in nearly everything but becoming disciples of Jesus Christ. We have filled the people with doctrines instead of Deity; we have given them manuals instead of Emmanuel. (36)

Three and a half years of undiluted Jesus will produce in us what it did in them: the kingdom of God! (37)

The eternal One who established His kingdom in men two millennia ago is fully capable of producing it in us today. All we need is undiluted, uninhibited Jesus. All we need are hearts that will not be satisfied with something or someone less than Him. (37)

If we argue church government and peripheral doctrines, we will miss completely the true purpose of the church, which is to make disciples of Jesus. (37)

After we recognize that the goal is not ministry but slavery, we will begin to see the power of Christ restored to the church. (37)

The pattern for leadership in the years ahead is simple: Leaders must be individuals whose burning passion is conformity to Jesus Christ. (37)

God can use practically any church structure if the people in that congregation are genuinely seeking Him. (38)

The outward form is not the issue with the Almighty; the true issue is the posture of the human heart before Him. (38)

Is it not true that the greater the sense of emptiness within us, the stronger is our hunger for God? (38)

We need to become a people whose heart's passion is to seek God until Christ Himself is actually formed within us (see Gal. 4:19). (39)

The Lord calls us to pay the same price, do the same works and possess the exact same benefits from prayer that Jesus did. (39)

Chapter 6

Our call is to possess that love of God which reaches into eternity and brings the glory and Person of Christ into His earthly house. (41)

In this maturation process there will come a point when within your heart love for God will take ascendancy over mere intellectual or doctrinal understanding. (42)

Genuine love for God is an unrelenting hunger. (43)

Let us also understand we will not find His fullness by seeking Him merely in convenient times and comfortable places. Rather our quest is a determined, continual pilgrimage which will not end until He is disclosed to us (see Phil. 3:12). (43)

This is the greatest motivation for seeking the Lord: The time will come when you find Him! (45)

We all want the Lord, but only the bride will go so far as to find Him and bring Him back to the house. (46)

He sees your repentance as your preparation for Him—His bride making herself ready. (46)

We have many tasks, even responsibilities, which have come from heaven. However, the need of our soul is to be with Jesus. (47)

Chapter 7·

It is possible for Christ's church to be so properly aligned with heaven that the Holy Spirit actually displaces the powers of darkness over our cities. (51)

During these past years God has had His church "at the quarry," shaping the leaders, preparing their hearts to become part of the house of the Lord. (52)

Together with their congregations these servants of God are building their churches, not upon the typical American base of self-promotion and human enterprise, but upon a substructure of corporate, citywide prayer and Christian love. (52)

When the Lord builds the house, *then* the Lord will guard the city. (54)

Ministers in churches are beginning to build together, training individuals from their congregations to go to other churches in the city where together the entire local Christian community is being built up. (56)

Ultimately, how will the house of the Lord differ from current Christianity? (56)

Where the house of the Lord is built, the protection of the Lord will be felt. (56)

Chapter 8

The redemptive power of God is released when people forgive each other. (59)

Perhaps nothing so typifies the transforming, cleansing power of God as that which is experienced when a soul receives forgiveness. (59)

Whenever pardon is abundantly given, there is a definite and occasionally dramatic release of life against the powers of death in the heavenly places. (60)

Forgiveness is the very spirit of heaven removing the hiding places of demonic activity from the caverns of the human soul. (62)

The power released in forgiveness is actually a mighty weapon in the war to save our cities. (62)

Whenever any relationship exists outside the shelter of covering love, it degenerates into a system of mutual expectations and unwritten laws to which we all become debtors. (63-64)

Whenever we are unforgiving, we are also reacting. Those un-Christlike reactions to offenses become our sin before God. (64)

The redemptive plan of God was this: If the Israelites set free their slaves, they would not be taken as slaves. If they showed mercy, He would show Himself merciful as well. The destruction of their cities would be averted, for "mercy triumphs over judgment" (James 2:13). (64)

Any society that hardens its heart toward mercy opens its heart toward hell. (65)

Where there is a decrease of love there will be an increase of demonic activity in our relationships. (66)

Chapter 9

There are things which make for peace. Pastors and their congregations must repent of the independence, spiritual pride and insecurities which have kept them isolated from each other. God has wonderful, awesome plans for our cities. But the substructure of these "things which make for peace" is the citywide church becoming a house of prayer. (72)

The only way we can stand victorious before our enemies is if we kneel humbly before our Lord together. (72)

Even now many large cities in the United States and Europe stand in the balance as to whether or not they will turn toward God or become places of utter darkness, great despair and destruction. (72-73)

God has placed the responsibility for our cities upon our shoulders! (73)

Chapter 10

Although calamities will become more devastating before the return of Christ, we must be assured of this: Even in His wrath God is always remembering mercy (see Hab. 3:2). (76)

The righteousness and sanctification that the living, holy church produces in a society can literally preserve that society from much of the evil which might otherwise destroy it. (76)

I am not preparing for *what* is going to happen but *who*. The bride is not making herself ready for a "date," but a marriage. (76-77)

The first phase of God's "vengeance" upon the world is aimed at releasing His elect from oppression. (77)

Whether it was with William Booth or John and Charles Wesley in England, Martin Luther in Germany or Francis of Assisi in Italy, it has always been *through the elect* that the Lord has impacted and transformed society. (78)

The answer to the present condition in our nation is not new government programs or new policies, but New Testament Christianity—oaks of righteousness that are empowered with the redemptive mercy of God. (78)

Chapter 11

God does not hinder the healing of our land. Rather our apathy and unbelief keep us from grasping the potential offered to us in the gospel of Christ. Do not marvel that entire cities can be saved. The Scripture tells us that nations will come to our light and kings to the brightness of our rising (see Is. 60:1-3). (79)

Yes, Jesus spoke to entire cities and expected them to repent, and He expects cities today to repent as well. (80)

The strategy to win our cities is for the church to reveal Christ's life in power. Yes, the revelation of Christ in us as individuals, and the power of Christ displayed corporately through us, can turn our worst cities back toward God! (80)

The sacrifice of Christ provides for the salvation of all men, and since the Father Himself desires all men to be saved, heaven waits only for the church to act. (80)

One may say, But that was then. Our cities are worse now. They are beyond redemption. Not so. Jesus continued His rebuke of cities by saying, "If the miracles had occurred in Sodom which occurred in you, it would have remained to this day" (Matt. 11:23). Amazingly, Jesus said even Sodom could find repentance! (80)

When we picture cities, we tend to see skylines and factories, streets and schools. Jesus, however, sees people. (81)

So much of our contemporary teaching keeps alive the very nature Jesus calls us to crucify. (81)

The Father's goal is not merely to bless us but to transform us into the image of His Son. He desires to use us to turn our cities back to Him. But God has made no provision for the healing of our land apart from our becoming Christlike. (82)

There is a legitimate dimension of faith that is coming from God. It is motivated by love and guided by wisdom, and it is coming from heaven to capture our cities. (82)

Many Christians think knowing the promises is the same as obtaining them. True faith literally *obtains* the promises of God. (83)

If evil can enter our cities through our negligence, evil can leave through our diligence. (83)

We might ask, But does this fit into my eschatology? Our "eschatologies" can be an excuse for unbelief. The fact is that we do not know when Jesus is returning. (83)

Let us not look for the apostasy anywhere else but in the areas of our own hearts. (83-84)

In the midst of the most terrible of times, the greatest darkness, the Lord proclaims, "Arise, shine; for your light has come, and the glory of the Lord has risen upon you. (84)

Chapter 12

To exercise true discernment, whether it is in regard to a person, a city or a nation, we must look beyond what is obvious to perceive the ultimate call and purpose of God. As Jesus perceived the woman at the well (John 4:1-15), so we must look beyond the harlotry of our country into the call and purposes of God. (87)

We may argue about the future, but we cannot deny the past. Regardless of where you stand concerning America and its prophetic relationship to this verse, the United States has always been a strong and high tower to the oppressed of the earth. (87-88)

Freedom is a "container" in which debate, dissent—even godlessness—can exist. (88)

What America has provided for every man is not Christianity but *opportunity*. We must do the rest. In our free society the battle is ideological and spiritual—and relentless, because the same freedoms afforded us are given to our enemies. We have but to relax our effort and, as we have seen, wickedness prospers. (89)

The very same laws which protect our right to assemble and worship protect humanists and atheists as well. Yet we should not fear this arena of battle. Indeed, we enjoy the greatest advantage, for our message of salvation is more liberating, more worthy and more relative to mankind's needs than all that the world offers. But we must *live* the gospel to win our war. (89)

We must understand emphatically that we are not warring against the United States, but the spirits of darkness which have attacked this country. (89)

The Christian's battleground does indeed, at times, expand into the courts. But the real war zone is in the spirit and soul of our neighborhoods and cities. As Christians we must take the battle into the same arena in which it has been fought since the first century: prayer and witnessing for Jesus. (90)

When *Jesus* is lifted up—not doctrines, programs and buildings, but Jesus—men are drawn unto Him, and society changes. (90)

Chapter 13

The zeal which consumes us and the love which compels us is for our Father's house. Our goal, which we believe is God's goal, is to see the born-again church united under the blood of Christ. (93)

We believe God's purpose is not to break off national affiliations, but to heal and establish relationships locally. (94)

In truth, our focus is not on becoming leaders, but followers of Jesus; not on a new doctrine, but on obedience to the directives of Christ. (94)

Religious pride was the first stronghold to fall, enabling us, as pastors from different streams, to flow together. God help us that it not be the first sin to arise in this new stirring of His Spirit! (94)

If a church recognizes Jesus as Lord and the need to be spiritually reborn; if they hold to the truth of the Scriptures and long for the personal return of the Lord Jesus, then we receive them as our brethren. (94)

What is this apostolic anointing? In the same way a pastor is anointed to care unselfishly for his local congregation, so the apostolic anointing awakens local ministers and intercessors to work together in meeting the needs of the citywide body of Christ. (95)

Those anointed with this fresh oil appreciate and respect the diversity of ministry which is already resident in the leaders of the praying, citywide church. (95)

In spite of the problem of sin in the ministry, we should beware of setting up a premature or legalistic standard of accountability, lest we cut off the flow of grace to our work. (96)

This first stage is *relational*, where we are more concerned with our brethren's needs than their creeds. (96)

Not out of corporate board meetings, but out of corporate prayer and dependency upon the Lord come divine directives for the church. (97)

Humility tells us that no amount of our ingenuity, manipulation or money could build a house for the Creator. Whatever we build for Him has a measure of idolatry in it; we ultimately find ourselves worshipping the works of our hands. (97)

Brokenness, a repentant heart and a holy, trembling fear of God are the building materials of the house of the Lord. It is the Lord's building, a place where He can rest. (98)

The essence of prayer is a yearning for Jesus. It would be in keeping with the highest purposes of God that entire prayer meetings be devoted to seeking the Lord. (98)

Apostolic intercession also assumes a posture of spiritual responsibility to support and protect what is newly born and vulnerable. (98)

As this ministry grows there will be those upon whose "prayer shoulders" God places the burden for their cities They will not and cannot sleep without praying for their communities. They assume a place of responsibility for the condition of the region. They will see a direct correlation between personal prayer and the retreat of the enemy from their cities. (99)

Chapter 14

The eternal foundation of the church is the Lord Jesus Christ; we rest and build upon Him. It is wisdom to build the Lord's house with only Jesus in mind. (101)

We cannot separate what Jesus says from who Jesus is. Christ and His Word are one. (102)

Christ and His Word are inseparable. Jesus was not a man who became the Word but is the eternal Word who became a man. His very nature is the Word of God. And to reject or ignore what He says is to reject or ignore who He is. (102)

The building coae of the kingdom must be obedience to the words of Christ. (102)

Beloved, there is a storm coming; even now the sky has darkened and the first drops are falling. If we will endure, we must be built upon the rock. Please hear me: you cannot build your house in a storm. It is through the Spirit and words of Christ that the house of the Lord is built. (103)

Only His words and Spirit are capable of restructuring our souls so that, through conformity to His nature, the Father Himself can make His abode in us (John 14:23). It is this refashioning of our inner man that, upon maturity, establishes us corporately as the house of the Lord. (103)

If the cornerstone is not in place the whole building tends to tilt toward the way we happen to lean. (103)

When we seek to build upon a foundation other than Jesus, the results are everything but Jesus. Only Christ can create Christians. (104)

Chapter 15

The wisdom of God can take even a poor man, train him in the ways of the Lord and give him a strategy to deliver a city. (105)

The chaos of our cities is not greater than the chaos which covered the deep, formless, pre-creation void. God's wisdom brought creation to order, and His wisdom can bring the church back to order as well. (105-106)

What is "the fear of the Lord"? It is the human soul, having experienced the crucifixion of self and pride, now trembling in stark vulnerability before almighty God. (106)

It is the awe-inspiring wonder of man living in fellowship, not with his religion, but with his God. In such a state the obedient man is invincible. (106)

The enemy does not fear the church because the church does not fear the Lord? As the fear of the Lord returns to us, the terror of the Lord will be upon our enemies. (106)

The Lord's house is built by wisdom. It is established as we compassionately seek to understand the needs of our brethren. After it is built and established, then knowledge fills the rooms with riches. (106)

Wisdom knows what to speak and when to speak it. (107)

Presented by itself even knowledge about unity can be divisive. (107)

We can have all the right doctrines and still live outside the presence of God if our hearts are not right. (108)

The outcome of right doctrines is love—love that covers other

Christians and builds up the body of Christ; it forgives when offended and serves without hidden motives. It goes extra miles ungrudgingly. If our doctrines are not producing this kind of love, they are a smoke screen that will keep us separate and outside the house of the Lord. (108)

Without knowledge we will perish, but knowledge without love is itself a state of perishing. (108)

To build the right foundation of the city-church we must all be in agreement about Jesus and His command to love one another. Greater wisdom than this will not be given concerning building the house of the Lord. (108-109)

Our labors must be for Jesus, not self. It must be the love of Christ which compels us, not a desire to rise in prominence among men. (109)

We must be more willing to serve than to lead, more willing to be corrected than to teach. (109)

True wisdom is not stubborn but is willing to yield to other ministries and perspectives. It must be unyielding in regard to the deity and centrality of Christ and yet fully aware that God desires all men to be saved. (109)

While the wisdom of God is meek, it is also "unwavering, without hypocrisy." This is wisdom born out of vision, not organizational skills. It is unwavering because it sees that the builder of the house is Christ. It is genuine, "full of mercy and good fruits," overlooking mistakes, helping the weaker churches, disarming suspicion and fear with the credibility of Christ's unfailing love. (109-110)

Chapter 16

In a move of God some will be willing to die for what God is doing, and some will be eager to kill them. (111)

Ultimately the ability to discern whether a teaching is truly from God rests in our willingness to obey Him. (112)

For in a move of God the gray routine of life ends. Both good and evil gravitate toward a state of fullness, stimulating prophets and "pharisees" alike to their true natures. (112)

The "key" to unlocking the power of knowledge is obedience. (113)

It is to our shame that the devil desires men's souls more than does the church. Therefore we must realize that revival will not sweep our land until we possess Christ's passion for the lost. (113)

One of our primary objectives in connecting churches is that through our unity Jesus will be revealed. It is Christ's glorious presence in the church, in contrast to the increasing darkness in our cities, which will draw multitudes to Him. (113-114)

The will of God is escorted to the earth through prayer. It is as simple as this: Revival is an answer to prayer; if we do not pray, there will be no revival. (114)

The message that brings worldwide awakening is that which embodies what God is doing and proclaims what God is saying. (115)

A wonderful dawn is breaking upon the church. While we have grown under the same teachers and fought against the same enemies, to our amazement we are discovering, in different ways, that the Lord has been guiding us all to Himself. This, we believe, is the anointed truth which God is speaking: It is time for the house of the Lord to be built. As Jesus steps forth from His house, revival will break forth in many cities. (115-116)

Chapter 17

While the doctrines of Christianity can be taught, Christlikeness can only be inspired. (117)

There are many administrators but few examples of Christ; many teachers but few who walk as Jesus walked. (117)

Spiritual authority is nothing less than God Himself confirming our words with His power. The examples in the Scriptures are plain: Those who are raised up by God are backed up by God. (118)

As He did for Samuel, the Lord will let none of their words fall to the ground, for their words and their authority will be a manifestation of the living God Himself. (118)

When the church returns to teaching all that Jesus taught, our disciples will have authority to do all that Jesus did. (118)

Jesus lived in the deepest intimacies of the Father's love because He laid down His life for the sheep. If we will grow in true authority, we will do so by laying down our lives for His sheep. (119)

When we could easily fight and win, yet turn the other cheek; when we are unjustly opposed, yet quietly endure—at those moments spiritual authority is entering our lives. (119)

Jesus had a choice: legions of warring angels and immediate personal deliverance, or death on the cross and deliverance for the world. He chose to die. The willful decision to lay down our lives as Jesus did is the very path upon which true authority develops. (119)

Spiritual authority is the power and provision of God to invade and transform the temporal with the power of the eternal. (120)

Divine authority requires divine sanction. This sanction comes from passing the tests of love. (120)

When authority is administered without love, it degenerates into control. (120)

We will walk in either the true authority of love, the false authority of control or no authority at all. (120)

Since true authority is built upon love, its goal is to liberate, not dominate. Therefore, before one can truly move in spiritual authority he must be delivered from fear and its desire to control; he must be rooted and grounded in love. (120)

God has given us people so we may train them, not merely count them. Of this group those whom we inspire to live like Christ are actually the measure of our success, the test of our effectiveness in the ministry. (121)

As wide as our sphere of love is, to that extent we have spiritual authority. (121)

The testing ground of all spiritual things is love, for love alone purifies our motives and delivers us from the deceitfulness of self. (122)

David gained the skills to slay Goliath by defending his father's sheep from vicious predators; he did not learn these skills on the battlefield. He loved the sheep so much that he would even risk his life for them. So also we grow in authority as we protect our Father's sheep, the flock He has given us to love. (122)

Authority is muscle in the arm of love. The more one loves, the more authority is granted to him. If we love our cities and are willing to lay down our lives for them, God will enlarge our hearts, granting us authority to confront principalities and powers. (122)

If we are truly anointed in God's love, the price to see our cities saved is not too great, for it is the price love always pays: the willingness to die for what we care for. (122)

We have been in exile from the promises of God, but we are returning to rebuild the Lord's house. It is not a time to tear down the body of Christ; it is time to establish and to build up. (123)

Chapter 18

The Lord honored the dedication of [Solomon's] temple with a visible unveiling of His glory. How much more does He seek to reveal His glorious presence in His living temple, the church? (126)

The way into that glory, the preparation for it, is occurring now in our obedience to the Lord and in our becoming His house. (126)

The true house of the Lord is only revealed when the church, without regard to divisions, is fitted together. Only then can we truly become the temple of the Lord, "a dwelling of God in the Spirit." (127)

Chapter 19

More churches have been destroyed by the accuser of the brethren and its faultfinding than by either immorality or misuse of church funds. (131)

In an attempt to hinder if not altogether halt the next move of God, Satan has sent forth an army of faultfinding demons against the church. (132)

The faultfinder spirit's assignment is to assault relationships on all levels. (132)

Masquerading as discernment, this spirit will slip into our opinions of other people, leaving us critical and judgmental. (132)

If our thoughts are other than "faith working through love," we need to be aware that we may be under spiritual attack. (132)

What we do with what we see is the measure of Christlike maturity. (132)

The enemy's purpose in this assault is to discredit the minister so it can discredit his message. (133)

To mask the diabolical nature of its activity, the faultfinder will often garb its criticisms in religious clothing. Under the pretense of protecting sheep from a "gnat-sized" error in doctrine, it forces the flock to swallow a "camel-sized" error of loveless correction. (134)

The church needs correction, but the ministry of reproof must be patterned after Christ and not the accuser of the brethren. (134)

Even in the most serious corrections the voice of Jesus is always the embodiment of "grace and truth" (John 1:14). (135)

To find an indictment against the church, it is important to note the enemy must draw his accusations from hell. (135)

We cast down the accuser of the brethren by learning to pray *for* one another instead of preying *on* one another. (135)

We defeat the faultfinder when we emulate the nature of Jesus: as a lamb, Christ died for sinners; as a priest, He intercedes. (136)

With the same zeal that the faultfinders seek to unearth sin, those who will conquer this enemy must earnestly seek God's heart and His calling for those they would reprove. (138)

True correction will proceed with *reverence,* not *revenge* (138)

To be anointed with Christ's authority to rebuke we must be committed to men with Christ's love. (139)

If we are not determined to die for men, we have no right to judge them. (139)

In the house of the Lord criticism must be replaced with prayer, and faultfinding eliminated with a covering love. (139)

Chapter 20

Emerging from Christ-centered unity and Christ-initiated prayer will be God's unique strategy for our cities. (142)

The Word of God is a two-edged sword; that is, there are two aspects of the Word, each as sharp as the other. The first is the *established* will of God, which comes through knowing the Scriptures. The second is the *communicated* will of God, which comes through our relationship with the Lord. (143)

The disciple of Christ should note carefully: Our greatest spiritual growth occurs when no one is looking, when we feel even God has withdrawn from us. (143)

Christians need to accept that the Father is not squeamish about testing His sons and daughters. (143)

We think of warfare in terms of "binding and loosing," but the endorsement of heaven, which actually accomplishes what we have decreed, is established in the wilderness of temptation and weakness. (144)

There is no authority without Christlike character; no lasting deliverance without facing the enemy and defeating him with God's Word. (144)

Chapter 21

Truly, each church must maintain its individual "sheepfolds," the local fellowship, for the sense of family and continuity. We are compelled by God's love to provide a spiritual shelter to raise our "little ones." However, we must also be armed and ready to war on behalf of our brethren. (146)

Although we are divided by "tribes" (denominations), we are all part of the same spiritual nation. (146)

We have no authority over a foe *outside* of us if we are compromising with that foe *inside* of us. (147)

In the initial stages of our training, we will soon discover that the Lord is more concerned with establishing His presence in the church than He is with addressing the regional principalities and powers. For it is not until the nature of Christ is in us, and the voice of Christ is speaking through us, that the Spirit of Christ penetrates the heavenly places, displacing the spiritual darkness over an area. (147-148)

As God delivers us from our arrogance, we see that we are without understanding when we compare ourselves to ourselves. We are not called to judge one another but to "love one another." (151)

What God is doing today is much like the restoration of the Jews from their Babylonian captivity. (151)

God is indeed preparing an exceedingly great army. Through it He intends to pull down the strongholds in the cities. However, they must be *connected in Christ* before the Spirit will anoint them for effective spiritual warfare. (152)

It takes a citywide church to win the citywide war. (152)

One person's transformation from carnality to the image of Christ can revolutionize a church; the transformation of the citywide church into the image of Christ can revolutionize a city. (152)

Chapter 22

Only by studying Jesus Himself with a view toward our own personal transformation will the mystery of the church be solved and the purpose of God be accomplished. (154)

Let us ask ourselves: Are we doing what Jesus did? For whatever Jesus did, the Spirit-anointed church will do likewise. (154)

The fact is that, when the Prince of Peace came, the prince of darkness rose to meet Him: Satan was Jesus' adversary. (155)

With each new spiritual level attained there is a fiercer, more adept enemy awaiting us. (156)

Paul is stating here that through the yielded, obedient church the authority of Jesus is exhibited in militant and triumphant victory over all the power of the devil, even over principalities and powers in the heavenly places. (158)

At the end of the age the Lord has promised a shaking that will topple all things. (160)

God is going to remove the proud rulers of the earth and the demonic rulers from the heavenlies. (160)

We also are learning the Lord's "moves." We know Christ's humility is our armor, His love is our strength, and His forgiveness disarms demons. (160)

Chapter 23

Whenever a word from the Lord is spoken, expect that it will be contested by the devil. (164)

This battle will not be won merely with the procedure of "binding" and "loosing." It will be won with *Christlike character* and holding fast to the word God has spoken. (164)

Our only answer in this assault is that our words must be backed up by functional Christlikeness. (165)

Satan seeks to exploit our weaknesses; God seeks to establish, in the very area of our weaknesses, the nature of His Son. All things must be perceived and understood in light of this reality. (165)

Without sacrificing the boldness of our faith nor entering into false humility, our confession must be without exaggeration or presumptuous statements. (165)

Conclusion

There is a resolution to our present distress, but the answer lies in the bosom of the church and in the context of our doing the will of God. (167)

Our prayer is that you will hear God's heart for yourself and, joined with others of like vision, will help build the house of the Lord. (167)

A SPECIAL NOTE

Also available by the same author:

Holiness, Truth and the Presence of God, a powerful and penetrating study of the human heart and how God prepares it for His glory.

The Three Battlegrounds, an in-depth view of the three arenas of spiritual warfare: the mind, the church and the heavenly places.

A number of these messages are available on audio cassette. For a complete catalog, as well as a free subscription to Francis Frangipane's newsletter, please write:

Advancing Church Ministries
P.O. Box 10102
Cedar Rapids, IA 52410